T0311689

Cambridge Elements ≡

Elements in Religion and Monotheism
edited by
Paul K. Moser
Loyola University Chicago
Chad Meister
Bethel University

MONOTHEISM AND EXISTENTIALISM

Deborah Casewell
University of Bonn

CAMBRIDGE
UNIVERSITY PRESS

CAMBRIDGE
UNIVERSITY PRESS

University Printing House, Cambridge CB2 8BS, United Kingdom

One Liberty Plaza, 20th Floor, New York, NY 10006, USA

477 Williamstown Road, Port Melbourne, VIC 3207, Australia

314–321, 3rd Floor, Plot 3, Splendor Forum, Jasola District Centre,
New Delhi – 110025, India

103 Penang Road, #05–06/07, Visioncrest Commercial, Singapore 238467

Cambridge University Press is part of the University of Cambridge.

It furthers the University's mission by disseminating knowledge in the pursuit of education, learning, and research at the highest international levels of excellence.

www.cambridge.org
Information on this title: www.cambridge.org/9781108984799
DOI: 10.1017/9781108985307

First published 2022

A catalogue record for this publication is available from the British Library.

ISBN 978-1-108-98479-9 Paperback
ISSN 2631-3014 (online)
ISSN 2631-3006 (print)

Monotheism and Existentialism

Elements in Religion and Monotheism

DOI: 10.1017/9781108985307
First published online: March 2022

Deborah Casewell
University of Bonn
Author for correspondence: Deborah Casewell, deborahc@uni-bonn.de

Abstract: Existentialism is often seen and at times parodied as the philosophy of individuality, authenticity, despair, and defiance in a godless world. However, it cannot be understood without reference to religion and, in particular, the monotheism of Christianity. Even the existentialist slogan, 'existence precedes essence', is formulated in relation to monotheism. This Element will show that monotheism and existentialism are intertwined: they react to each other and share content and concerns. This Element will set out a genealogy of existentialist thought, explore key atheistic and theistic existentialists, and argue that there are productive conversations to be had as regards key concepts such as freedom and authenticity, relationality, and ethics.

Keywords: existentialism, God, religion, atheism, ontology

ISBNs: 9781108984799 (PB), 9781108985307 (OC)
ISSNs: 2631-3014 (online), 2631-3006 (print)

Contents

1 What Is Existentialism?

1.1 Definitions and Debates, Paradigms and Patterns

One problem with defining existentialism is that although there are many definitions, there is no definitive statement of what it is. This is maybe apt: after all, perhaps the most famous existentialist slogan is that existence precedes essence. So one should not bat an eyelid at existentialism preceding any particular definition of what it is. Another famous slogan is that man is nothing else but what he makes of himself, and certainly, it can be said that there are instances in which existentialism has been taken to be little more than what we make of it.

There have been enough attempts to define existentialism that they can themselves be sorted into various paradigms. One is to see existentialism in terms of family resemblance. However, this has often led to thinkers being forcibly adopted into this family rather than being naturally begotten members of it.[1] Thus, we find many members of this unhappy family unhappy in their own ways, all linked, usually through shared unhappiness, to existentialism. Yet enough differences remain that any cohesive account of existentialism is doomed, appropriately, to further unhappiness.

Amongst those seen as existentialists in the family resemblance sense are figures as diverse as Socrates, Augustine, Blaise Pascal, Friedrich Schelling, and G. W. F. Hegel, whose differences override their similarities. Søren Kierkegaard is particularly illustrative of this difficulty, existing almost as Schrödinger's existentialist: simultaneously the paradigmatic existentialist and not one at all. Whilst I would say that Nietzsche is not an existentialist, existentialism is unthinkable without him. Gabriel Marcel is claimed to have first used the term,[2] yet when he labelled Jean-Paul Sartre as an existentialist, Sartre rejected it. In turn, when Sartre labelled Marcel a Christian existentialist, he disavowed the philosophy. In that same lecture, 1945's 'Existentialism Is a Humanism', Sartre enveloped Martin Heidegger and Karl Jaspers into existentialism, resulting in Heidegger's repudiation of existentialism and Jaspers distancing his *Existenzphilosophie* from existentialism.[3]

---

[1] For instances of this, see Cooper 1990, 6–10, 2012, 28–30; Earnshaw 2006, 1–2; Flynn 2006, 8; Grimsley 1960, 1–11; Joseph et al. 2011, 3–4; Macquarrie 1972, 14–18; Reynolds 2006, 2–3; Warnock 1967, 1–2.

[2] Beauvoir reports that Marcel coined the term and that in 1943, she associated existentialism with Kierkegaard and Heidegger (Beauvoir 1962, 547–548; Contat and Rybalka 1974, 12).

[3] There is significant interplay between the terms existential, existentialism, and philosophy of existence. In German philosophy, they were largely, but not consistently, separated out: *existentiell* analysis explores the concrete, factual aspects of human existence; *Existentialphilosophie* analyses the ontological structures of human existence; and *Existenzphilosophie* analyses human

This lecture formed part of the so-called existentialist offensive and became foundational for public perceptions of existentialism. It is the source of the two definitions mentioned at the beginning of this Element. Yet Sartre came to regret his presentation of existentialism here, and its arguments were contested, not least by his collaborator in the offensive, Simone de Beauvoir. Their contemporary, Albert Camus, writing under similar influences and on similar themes, is often claimed as an existentialist despite his own fulsome disagreements with Sartre.

Existentialism was also a literary and cultural movement: Dostoevsky's novels figure prominently in discussions of existentialism; Marcel, Sartre, Beauvoir, and Camus wrote novels and plays that expressed their philosophical ideals and wrote on literary figures such as Jean Genet. For some authors, only certain works are considered existentialist: Tolstoy's *Death of Ivan Ilyich* is allowed, *War and Peace* and *The Kreutzer Sonata* are not.

If describing existentialism as a family only creates unhappiness, then one could define existentialism in an atmospheric sense.[4] Here, a number of concepts and conditions are set for what constitutes the atmosphere of existentialism. However, there is a sense of diminishing returns here as the conditions and concepts pile up, some of which cohere with each other and some of which do not. Flynn lists five key themes for existentialism: existence preceding essence, time being of the essence, humanism, freedom and responsibility, and ethical considerations as paramount (2006, 8). Yet this elides a number of other concepts that appear regularly in the existentialist literature: a focus on the absurdity of the world and of individual human existence within it, a rejection of a unified, given human nature or essence, seeing despair and anxiety as symptomatic of human existence, freedom as the key feature of the human condition, and a stress on revaluing and creating one's own values.[5] It also does not quite

---

existence in a non-objectifying manner less concerned with ontology. However, these terms were elided in the French reception into *philosophie existentielle* (Baring 2015).

[4] Judaken details a historical description rather than trying to find a definition, which he sees as contrary to true existentialism. Existentialism is therefore 'an interchange amongst a group of thinkers from different regions who came to share a vocabulary for naming a set of problems in the shared setting of modernity' (2012, 2). Debates also range over to what extent existentialism can be described as a philosophy. Kaufmann argues that it is instead 'a label for several widely different revolts against traditional philosophy', where the one essential feature is a 'perfervid individualism' (1995, 11). Dreyfus emphasises 'opposition to the philosophical tradition' (Dreyfus 2006, 137) alongside the centrality of despair. Pierre Hadot sees aspects of existential thinkers such as Nietzsche and Heidegger as being concerned with a Socratic account of philosophy as a way of life, which Flynn also notes. Solomon echoes this, claiming that 'nothing could be further from the existential attitude than attempts to define existentialism, except perhaps a discussion about the attempts to define existentialism' (1974, xix). That judgement I leave to the reader.

[5] A small survey: Grene sees that Jaspers and Marcel are not proper existentialists as they lack 'the terrible realisation of dread as the core of human life' (1948, 138). Murdoch includes freedom,

draw out the connections between the concepts. For example, although existentialist freedom and responsibility may be overwhelming, they are also the possibility of authentic existence as that must be chosen by the individual rather than given to them by someone or something external.

As I shall explore in the Section 3, other attempts to define existentialism have been made genealogically, ethically, and sociologically. In order to give a clear account of the relationship of monotheism to existentialism, I will distinguish between proto-existentialism and existentialism proper. The former category includes thinkers who I consider to be forerunners to, and influential on, existentialism without themselves being existentialists. In the latter category, I include thinkers who explicitly describe themselves as existentialists. And to return to the beginning of this Element, I will focus on thinkers who explicitly engage with the ontological statement that existence precedes essence.

The distinction between the proto-existentialist and the existentialist proper is not always easy to maintain. It is the aim of this Element to illustrate why. Existentialism is incredibly broad but also quite specific, and teasing out why exactly it is both will show how a concern with monotheism can be enfolded within these definitions. I will be able to incorporate a history of how monotheism acted as a spur, as well as a challenge, to questions seen as particular to existentialism: questions of value, existence, and the human condition.

This Element does not seek a new definition of existentialism – there are enough of them out there. It does, however, argue for a new understanding of existentialism. This new understanding adds another concept to the atmospheric definition and strengthens the branches in the family tree. I will argue that a relation and concern with God is part of the definition of existentialism. I will also argue that those who base their philosophy on God can be understood as existentialists as much as those who reject God: even, and especially, if they argue that existence precedes essence. As I am arguing that existentialism proper always relates to that statement, I will make the point that this statement itself is one that is inherently concerned with monotheism. The inclusion of this

---

values, and the will to power (1999). Walter Kaufmann argues that existentialism shows a concern with the dizziness of freedom that comes from a conception of the self that 'is essentially intangible and must be understood in terms of possibilities, dread, and decisions . . . my choice is made in fear and trembling'. These motifs are 'central in all so-called existentialism' (1995, 17). Barrett lists 'anxiety, death, the conflict between the bogus and the genuine self, the faceless man of the mass, the experience of the death of God' (1958, 9). Malpas argues that existentialism pertains to the structures of human existence (2012, 293). Other broad studies of existentialism focus on a shared set of concerns or a particular atmosphere. Wahl argues that there is an atmosphere that pervades them and that 'all definitions are more or less inadequate' (Wahl 1969, 3). There is, however, a subject that 'is oriented towards possibility', who '*is* choice, freedom, projects, uniqueness, subjective truth, paradox' (89).

concept enables me to make distinctions between the proto- and existentialist proper that are attentive to genealogical accounts of existentialism whilst not tying it to particular reception histories.

1.2 Is Existentialism an Atheism?

The popular view of existentialism is that it is resolutely atheistic. Yet if there is one religion that existentialism engages with, both positively and negatively, it is Christianity.[6] To put it simply: the charge is that monotheism entails a set, unchanging essence or nature for both God and humanity. God is the stable, unchanging substance that grounds human existence. Humanity therefore has a set essence and purpose given to it by God. The statement that existence precedes essence is a rejection of this. The focus on monotheism in this text will explore how questions of being and essence relate to existence and whether existence preceding essence is compatible with monotheism.

As old scholarship has noted and recent scholarship has underscored, a preoccupation with God is not merely an undercurrent in existentialist philosophies, explicitly atheistic or otherwise. This preoccupation comes out in varying ways, which often mix in and amongst each other. Perhaps there is a debt to religious accounts of the human condition and existence or a sense in which the concept of God either provides stability or represents a psychological or ontological horizon; maybe there are tensions between the implied stability that monotheism provides in contrast to the finite, limited temporality of existence.[7] Even, and perhaps especially, in accounts that reject monotheism, the trappings cannot be simply cleared away.

Despite this, concern with God is rarely seen as a defining feature of existentialism. Instead, in the popular vision of existentialism, God is *de trop*. It is this reading that I wish to contest in this Element, both through bringing out

---

[6] Although there is some engagement between Buddhism and existentialism in the Kyoto School, their focus was more on Meister Eckhart and Heidegger's use of nothingness than questions of essence and being associated with Christianity.

[7] Wahl notes that philosophies of existence all relate to transcendence. Heidegger ends up with a (slightly pagan) view of the holy and Sartre attributes to humanity the freedom of a God and an impotent desire to be God (1969). Kaufmann remarks that 'religion has always been existentialist' in that it is 'preoccupied with suffering, death, and dread, with care, guilt, and despair' (1975, 49). Martin's opinion is that 'even among the atheists, who today are better remembered, the questions addressed by existentialism look suspiciously akin to religious (or perhaps better, spiritual) questions' (2006, 188). Stewart notes the desire of Camus to 'preserve the actual content of Christian ethics and values whilst rejecting their metaphysical grounding' (2010, 181). Whilst Warnock remarks that God's existence makes little difference to existentialist theory as 'in practice there is no help to be found in *believing in God*' (1970, 134), Grene notes that the absence of God in Sartre is what makes his philosophy possible (1948, 42), and Cochrane notes that Sartre's existentialism is 'tortured by the thought that God might not be and yet must be' (1956, 11).

the monotheistic impetus behind and within existentialism and by detailing how the atheistic existentialists are not quite able to escape from God. After all, certain key existentialist concepts hinge on monotheism: absurdity, for instance, arises from the lack of inherent meaning in existence that God would grant. Yet the centrality of absurdity in existentialism comes from Kierkegaard, who was very much a theist: indeed, belief arises by virtue of the absurd. Atheistic existentialists may argue that God's existence limits human freedom by giving humanity a nature and an essence, but Marcel's philosophy, grounded on God, contradicts that judgement. The non-theistic thinkers chiefly associated with existentialism, namely Sartre, de Beauvoir, and Camus, are not casual about the non-existence of God nor its effects.

Therefore, a particular concern with God marks existentialism. The existence of God, the limits, possibilities, and problems of monotheism are foundational to the formation of distinctively existentialist understandings of ontology, freedom, and ethics. Existentialists proper, those who found their philosophy on the statement that existence precedes essence, will formulate their ontology differently depending on that statement's relation to God. That ontology will then ground their understanding of freedom; that freedom will define their ethics in relation to other people. The majority of those who have been subsumed into the existentialist family or enveloped in the existentialist atmosphere have a relationship with monotheism. That relationship is such that even when it is reacted against negatively, it is illustrative and even foundational, and when positively, it opens up new possibilities. Existentialism cannot be understood without reference to monotheism, although the engagement is such that, again, there is no single definitive approach.

I will explore the relationship between existentialism and monotheism in three key areas: genealogy, ontology, and ethics. The questions and concepts that arise in discussing these incorporate accounts of the nature and quality of human existence. These include how to understand freedom and responsibility: both individually and in relation to others, alongside questions of the primacy of activity or passivity. The following section explores the genealogy of existentialism proper by looking at six proto-existentialists: Augustine, Pascal, Nietzsche, Kierkegaard, Heidegger, and Jaspers. The majority of these proto-existentialists are theistic and grapple with the nature of human existence in relation to God. Although some of these thinkers reject theism, they still engage with monotheism and its implications for human existence, and explore what human existence is in light of that lack. Their own navigation of the relationship of God to existence provides the essential context for exploring how the statement that existence precedes essence is one that is concerned with monotheism.

Section 3 will explore three thinkers associated with both existentialism proper and atheism: Sartre, Beauvoir, and Camus. This section will look at how Sartre and Beauvoir came to develop and define existentialism and how Camus is connected with and yet separate from existentialism proper. In their definitions and rejections of existentialist concepts, the way in which each thinker grapples with monotheism will be explored. Sartre's philosophy grapples with God as an impossible ideal, whereas Beauvoir's explicitly ethical existentialism rejects God as a ground in favour of freedom. That, however, raises issues of abstraction and instability. Camus's famous Sisyphean defiance belies his enduring engagement with Christianity. The similarities and differences between these three thinkers, on questions of human nature and existence, ethics, and monotheism, will show that existentialism, even in its most proper form, cannot be separated from a concern with God. Indeed, none of these thinkers found a way, successfully, of being saints without God.

Section 4 will explore three theists whom I consider to be existentialists proper: Gabriel Marcel, Nikolai Berdyaev, and Paul Tillich. They all engage with the premise that existence precedes essence, and they all respond to the atheistic existentialists. Gabriel Marcel's thought sparked the existentialism that was popularised by Sartre, but his philosophy challenges the conclusions of Sartre and Beauvoir. Although the key themes of Nikolai Berdyaev's thought developed through a different lineage from their phenomenological reception, he embraces himself as an existentialist, finding creativity and freedom sourced in, rather than opposed to, God. Paul Tillich takes seriously the ontological challenges of atheistic existentialism. These thinkers all develop, in differing ways and through their different theological traditions, theistic existentialisms that accept, but then transcend, existentialist visions of human existence and its condition. They show as well that monotheism can help, rather than hinder, human freedom and existence.

I will conclude by identifying and exploring three key areas in which monotheism is concerned with existentialism, positively and negatively. These are passivity and activity, freedom and responsibility, and ontology and relationality.

2 Climbing the Existentialist Tree: Six Proto-Existentialists

Figure 1 depicts Emanuel Mounier's existentialist tree. This early genealogy of existentialism emphasises its religious heritage. Whilst the roots of the tree draw from Christians and Ancient Greeks, the body and many of the branches are formed of religious thinkers. In his *Introduction*, amongst themes such as the contingency of human being, the failure of reason in the face of human

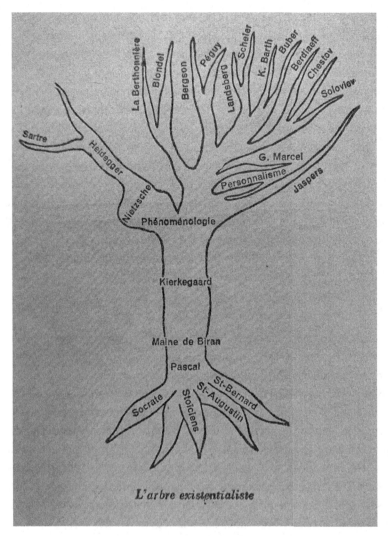

Figure 1 l'arbre existentialist (Mounier 1946)

existence, anguish at responsibility, the agony of choice, and truth as subjectivity, Mounier also identifies a stress on a divine inner transcendence that grounds human relationality. This may be why Nietzsche, Heidegger, and Sartre are placed on their own rather lonely, diverging branch.

Mounier's tree is useful: it shows that the genealogy of existentialism was being written and debated as existentialism itself made its steps into popularity. The following section explore six thinkers on this tree. Perhaps the overwhelming similarity that unites the following, quite disparate thinkers is that they describe human existence as characterised by anxiety and despair. There are other features of their thought that entail they lean more into agreement than not, such as a focus on the self and the individual, and their lack of unity with the world and others. It is from these disjunctions that feelings of anxiety and despair arise.

Yet I would hesitate to refer to the following thinkers simply as existentialists or to overly stress the anxiety and despair. Often the following thinkers are smuggled into existentialism, but I am loathe to do so here. I would instead say that atmospheric aspects of existentialism are present in their thought, often as a part of the whole. This distinguishes them from the existentialist proper, whose thought I see as orientated more overtly around the premise that existence precedes essence. However, giving a clear account of themes that are taken up in existentialism and their treatment in thinkers who have been brought into the existentialist canon is helpful. Whilst existentialism has been observed to stretch back to Socrates and Plato, in keeping with my monotheistic concern, this survey of proto-existentialists begins with Augustine.

2.1 Augustine (354–430)

Although Augustine's thought is diffused throughout Western philosophy, it is particularly pertinent to existentialism. His presentation of the human condition is key to his influence on and incorporation into existentialism.[8] His autobiographical analysis of human existence in the *Confessions* presents the self that has 'become to myself a vast problem' (1961, IV.4): restless, anxious, and fallen, searching for meaning and purpose in a world filled with distractions and temptations. Existence is marked by the disjunction of the self and its idea of itself to the world that surrounds it, its expectations, and the others that dwell within it. The self conflicts with and fails them, as it does also with God. God, as the source of being and goodness, calls the self to that goodness but is hidden behind the distractions, cares, and concerns of everyday life.

Having been created by God from nothing, the self is situated between God and nothingness. The self therefore lacks ontological wholeness, unlike God. The lack and instability in human nature means that whilst we are created to desire and seek happiness in God as the source of our being, we tend towards sin, turning away from the source of goodness and towards nothingness.[9] Our

---

[8] Wahl writes that Augustine 'replaced pure speculation with a kind of thinking closer to the person, the individual' (1949, 9).

[9] (2003, X.xx.29). Augustine writes that 'man did not fall away to the extent of losing all being; but when he had turned towards himself his being was less real than when he adhered to him who exists in a supreme degree. And so, to abandon God and to exist in oneself, that is to please oneself, is not immediately to lose all being; but it is to come nearer to nothingness' (2003, XIV. xiii.572–573).

will turns towards sin through a self-deception that is sourced in our pride. Pride presents us with an ameliorated picture of ourselves, which prevents us from truly engaging in self-examination. We can only examine ourselves truthfully by turning our love and regard from ourselves towards God. We are then able to see and know ourselves clearly and truthfully.

Turning towards God is Augustine's solution to our restlessness, anxiety, and despair. We find our rest in the fullness of God's goodness and being rather than entrenching ourselves further into nothingness and self-regard.[10] It is in God that 'our good abides and it has no blemish' (1961, IV.16). Augustine's vision of human existence outside of God contains the germ of existentialism. His description of human existence and the human condition prior to salvation: as fallen, individual, anguished, and self-deceptive, will re-emerge in later proto-existentialists as well as in existentialism proper. Augustine's philosophy offers us a relief from fraught human nature, a rest in the being of God. As we shall see in later thinkers, the possibility of rest or the promise of fullness becomes either impossible or another deception.

2.2 Blaise Pascal (1623–1662)

Due to his association with Jansenism, Pascal is seen to stand within the Augustinian tradition. His own philosophical work moves in different directions, and although there are similarities to Augustine's vision of existence, Pascal anchors the existentialist vision in other ways. Nietzsche, who was deeply dismissive of Augustine, lauded Pascal, listing him as amongst those philosophers whose blood mingles with his in sacrifice and from whom and on whom 'I will accept judgement . . . [and] fix my eyes and see theirs fixed on me' (Nietzsche 1996, 408). Sartre read Pascal in his youth, and referring to his wager Beauvoir's student diaries comment that Pascal formulates the only true, unsolvable problem, that 'I would want to believe in something – to meet with total exigency – to justify my life. In short, I would want God' (Beauvoir 2006, 262).

Pascal's thought dwells on the human condition, his thought emphasising more fervently than Augustine's the impossibility of human effort and true self-knowledge. Channelling Socrates, he sees we are enjoined to begin the process of knowing by knowing ourselves. However, this is frustrated by our very nature as the human condition is that of 'inconstancy, boredom, anxiety' (1995, L24/B127). In this boredom, one 'feels his nothingness, his desertion,

---

[10] 'Confronted with the disclosure of that anxiety which relates to nothing in the world but arises from his own being, man has an alternative to that flight into an inauthentic existence of surrender to the world – namely recourse to God, who is the ground of being, Creator of both man and the world' (Macquarrie 1955, 71).

his insufficiency, his dependence, his weakness, his emptiness'. When self-knowledge is attempted 'immediately from the depth of his heart will emerge ennui, gloom, sadness, distress, vexation, despair which inhibits this' (L622/B131).

In a frequently quoted fragment, Pascal laments this contradictory, irreconcilable, and irresolvable state of humanity:

> What a chimera then is man! What a novelty! What a monster, what a chaos, what a contradiction, what a prodigy! Judge of all things, imbecile worm of the earth; depositary of truth, a sink of uncertainty and error; the pride and refuse of the universe! (L131/B434)

Yet, despite the fact that 'man is only a reed, the weakest in nature', he is a 'reed that thinks' (L6/347).

In Pascal's measure, we are such because we are caught between two impossible poles. We are 'a nothingness with respect to the infinite, an everything with respect to nothingness', and therefore 'a place between everything and nothing' (L199/B72). We also long for love and respect, both from ourselves and others. Yet this is an impossible longing as we cannot know the truth about ourselves. Suffering from our self-deceptive narratives, we narrate our own self to ourselves and others, desiring a complete narrative and wholeness. However, instead we constantly come up against the 'nothingness of our own being' (L806/B147).

What can satisfy us if we can never find satisfaction from ourselves or others? Only God and the fullness of God's being and love can satisfy our longing. But our nature prevents us from seeking out the correct solution to our inherent problem. Therefore, Pascal sees that before God, we must be passive and accept our nothingness, our fallenness, and the inadequacy of our attempts to overcome this. Only then we may be granted grace, but this is not at all guaranteed. Even our rest is hemmed in by anxiety and despair, compounded by our impotence in the face of existence.[11] Pascal's vision of human existence and his response to it foreshadow several conundrums that will plague existentialism proper: whether humanity's passivity is something to be rejected or worked around and whether truly authentic existence can be given or can only be chosen.

2.3 Søren Kierkegaard (1813–1855)

We turn from the more distant ancestors to the man described often as the Father of Existentialism. Kierkegaard is illustrative as a thinker who is not as directly

---

[11] This lack of certainty is in part as Pascal's religious thought sought to mediate between the casuistry of the contemporary Jesuits and the limited grace of the Calvinists.

dependent on the Augustinian lineage and yet is tangled within it. Also known as the 'Pascal of the North',[12] he dwells on similar themes in his exploration of the human condition and the relationship between the finite and the infinite. Like Augustine, he sees that the 'path to authentic selfhood' is one that can only be realised in relation to God.[13] The spurs for Kierkegaard's philosophy of existence lie however more within the German Idealist tradition, drawing from and reacting against the philosophies of Friedrich Schelling and Georg Hegel.

The late thought of Schelling certainly contains existentialist notes. Kierkegaard was in attendance at Schelling's 1841–1842 lectures in Berlin. He initially enjoyed them but then, like his co-attendees Friedrich Engels and Mikhail Bakunin, found them deeply frustrating and disappointing. In these lectures, Schelling differentiates between negative philosophy and positive philosophy. Negative philosophy is a philosophy that sees that the Absolute, or God, can be known to the human mind, whereas positive philosophy argues that it is beyond thought. Instead of the static, pantheistic absolute essence of Schelling's earlier *Identitätsystem*, what we know of God is always

> just knowledge which is coming to be, because the true god himself is for consciousness not the existing god, but always just the god who is coming to be, who precisely as such is also called the living god, forever just the god who appears, who must always be called to and captured as an appearance is captured. The knowledge of the true god remains, thus, always a *demand*.
> (Schelling 1989, 177)[14]

Whereas Kierkegaard's response to the Hegelianism rampant in the philo-sophical and religious climate in Denmark was of a devastating parody. Kierkegaard shows that the stages of Spirit in attaining the Absolute Idea, sublated in the progression of logic, are in fact utterly inadequate and useful only as a thought experiment. Instead, Kierkegaard sees that the real question of existence begins where the system ends. Kierkegaard's leap of faith both transcends and contains the aesthetic and ethical stages, whereas Hegel's stages are ever the triumph of reason.

Kierkegaard's *oeuvre* is complex: he not only wrote prodigiously but also practised pseudonymous authorship and ironic, indirect communication. The

---

[12] This is often due to them being detailed as fideists, a term that does a grave injustice to their complex engagement with questions of truth, subjectivity, and rationality. However, other texts view their positions as outsiders or as detailing a divided self as common ground on which to draw them together.

[13] For discussions of the similarities but ultimately differences, see Paffenroth et al. 2017.

[14] Pattison lists the existentialist themes in Schelling's late thought: 'the agonistic character of freedom and its association with suffering and anxiety, the priority of the unthinkable over the thinkable, an emphasis on the crucial element of will and of the continuing role of the irrational in the economy of consciousness' (Pattison 1999, 18).

pseudonymity both conceals and reveals. In distancing the author from his works, it may allow for the author to engage in greater self-revelation. The indirectness of the communication, filtered through pseudonyms and characters, entails that the reader has to grasp the truth as their own rather than taking it as given. However, this has complicated the reception of Kierkegaard. For example, *Either/Or* is edited by one pseudonym and contains essays authored by different pseudonyms. One of these texts, the novella *The Seducer's Diary*, was published separately in France in 1929. However Kierkegaard's works do have perennial concerns, and his influence on existentialism can be brought out through two themes: his discussions of anxiety and despair in relation to authentic and inauthentic existence, and his account of truth as subjectivity.

Discussion of the former tends to revolve around two particular texts. In the companion texts *The Concept of Anxiety* and *The Sickness Unto Death,* Kierkegaard writes on original sin, noting his journals that discussions of it lack a primary category: anxiety, which is 'the essential determinant' (Kierkegaard 1967–1978, i.94). *The Concept of Anxiety*, authored by one Vigilius Haufniensis (the watchman), redresses this through an examination of the individual consciousness. It explores the relationship between sin and freedom in relation to the account of the fall in Genesis. Positing that each sin is an original sin, coming into the world in a qualitative leap, the author reasons that the psychological conditions for that to take place are 'a sympathetic antipathy and an antipathetic sympathy', or anxiety (Kierkegaard 1980, 42).

Anxiety is the bare state of humanity because humanity is fundamentally not at one with itself. To be a self is to be an irreconcilable synthesis of the finite and the infinite. However, this anxiety is the condition of our freedom; it is 'freedom's actuality as the possibility of possibility' (155). This text does not seek to explain or justify the fall but observes instead that our freedom is our anxiety: our disjunction enables possibilities and choices. Anxiety is that 'dizziness of freedom' where we want to posit the synthesis between the finite and infinite, where 'freedom now looks down into its own possibility, laying hold of finiteness to support itself' (61).

In Anti-Climacus's *The Sickness Unto Death,*[15] despair is added to the experiences of the free self. In despair 'there is an interplay of finitude and infinitude, of the divine and the human, of freedom and necessity' (Kierkegaard 1983, 145): again the self is fundamentally irreconcilable. The self seeks out stability and wholeness, but it cannot be a stable being. Instead, 'the self is a relation that relates itself to itself or is the relation's relating itself to itself in

---

[15] A prior pseudonym Kierkegaard used was Johannes Climacus, the name of the sixth-/seventh-century monk who authored the *Ladder of Divine Ascent,* detailing how one raises oneself to God through ascetic practice.

the relation; the self is not the relation but is the relation's relating itself to itself' (13). We are unable to 'become' ourselves because we cannot 'be' ourselves. We know that we are free, and possibilities dance before us each day. But choosing one possibility will always shut off the others.

Yet the despair that we exist in, with its freedom and possibilities, is also the condition for authentic existence. Despair, as the disjunction that comes from our synthesis of finitude and infiniteness, is eternity's claim upon us as much as it is eternity's greatest concession to us (21). A solution to this despair is found in God, in relation to whom the self can actually become itself. The 'conscious synthesis of infinitude and finitude that relates itself to itself' must become itself, which 'can be done only through the relationship to God' (29–30). God offers a new kind of possibility as the antidote to despair, as 'for God everything is possible at every moment' (39–40).

However, this can be a hard pill to swallow, as in despair the self does not seek solace, but instead to make itself into itself. It

> wants to have the honour of this poetic, masterly construction, the way it has understood itself. And yet, in the final analysis, what it understands by itself is a riddle; in the very moment when it seems that the self is closest to having the building completed, it can arbitrarily dissolve the whole thing into nothing. (69–70)

If we make this move before God or with knowledge of God, we sin. Sin is thus 'intensified weakness or intensified defiance: sin is the intensification of despair' (77). Therefore, for Anti-Climacus, 'the opposite to being in despair is to have faith' (49). Faith is an act of repetition: choosing again and again to be in relationship to the God for whom everything is possible.

Faith is always an individual, subjective act. Kierkegaard is wary of the social, seeing that society tends towards conformity, towards levelling. Levelling is the reduction of the differences of individuals and a limitation of their desire to make existential choices, moving them into predetermined roles and opinions. As the crowd is the untruth in which the individual loses themselves, Kierkegaard focuses on and calls instead to the individual to make their own choice on existence, to choose the 'truth which is true for me . . . the idea for which I can live or die' (Kierkegaard 1967–1978, 5:5100).

Truth is not objective knowledge but a relation. Formulated philosophically in his *Concluding Unscientific Postscript*, 'when the question about truth is asked subjectively, the individual's relation is reflected upon subjectively. If only the how of this relation is in truth, the individual is in truth, even if he in this way were to relate himself to untruth' (Kierkegaard 1982, 99). Yet this is a risk: belief in the truth of the transcendent God, in particular, takes us out into 'the mortal danger of lying out on 70,000 fathoms of water, and only there finding God' (232). This terrifying relation to the transcendent God is underscored in Kierkegaard's treatment of Abraham in *Fear and Trembling*, who, in the face of being asked to sacrifice his son, believes by virtue of the absurd that he will receive him back. Only through such a leap are we able to make the move from the finite to the infinite and return, receiving ourselves back in the act of losing it: becoming the knight of faith rather than the knight of infinite resignation.

As the Father of Existentialism, Kierkegaard's thought, alongside Heidegger and Jaspers, evinces aspects more akin to the stricter account of existentialism proper. The solace that God provides is through possibility, and whilst there is rest, it is through possibility. This reflects an ontological shift post-Hegel, where God's being is a process of becoming rather than a static essence. In this sense, Kierkegaard thus accords with the broader, atmospheric sense of existentialism. Although the questions of essence and existence are raised in his thought, the focus is more on infiniteness rather than on the ontology of possibility. Indeed, Kierkegaard's reception, both immediate and mediated, emphasises more his treatment of freedom, anxiety and despair, and truth as subjectivity.

2.4 Friedrich Nietzsche (1844–1900)

As noted previously, Nietzsche held Pascal in high esteem, similarly appreciated Dostoevsky, and may well have done the same to Kierkegaard.[16] His relationship to Christian thought otherwise tends towards profound hostility. Augustine, for example, is derided as conflicted and weak, and the promise of reconciliation and rest in his thought result from that weakness. This surrender of the human life and activity is done in favour of a vision of happiness that, in reality, 'corresponds to that of a medicine and a mentality of pacification', a 'narcotic' (Nietzsche 2001a, 200).[17]

Instead, life should embrace vitality, will, and rejoice in strength and instinct. Nietzsche's first work, *The Birth of Tragedy*, sets out three different ways of existing: the Dionysian, which stands in contrast to the Apollonian, and is then in turn obscured by the Socratic. The Apollonian instinct upholds reason, harmony, order, and balance. It is a philosophy of order, whereas the Dionysian rejoices in life and the will, appealing to emotions, instincts, disorder, and beauty. That immediacy and truth are lost with the rise of the Socratic

---

[16] In *Twilight of the Idols*, Nietzsche writes of Dostoevsky as a *'profound'* human being, the only psychologist 'from whom I had something to learn' (Nietzsche 1990, 109). He had been alerted to Kierkegaard's thought in 1888 by Georg Brandes, but his collapse in 1889 ended his working life.

[17] Although see Michalski 2013 and Mulhall 2005 for an account of Nietzsche as more Augustinian than he would like to admit.

the 'unshakeable belief that rational thought, guided by causality, can penetrate to the depths of being, and that it is capable not only of knowing but even of *correcting* being' (Nietzsche 1993, 73). Against this controlling instinct, Nietzsche calls for humanity to 'dare to be tragic men, for you will be redeemed' (98).

This emphasis on instinct, life, will, and power is, throughout his later works, contrasted with structures and morality that subdue it. In *Beyond Good and Evil* and *Genealogy of Morals,* Nietzsche develops his account of how this morality came to be and offers a glimpse of what could lie beyond it for those who dare. Whilst the will to power is the *'primordial fact* of all history' (Nietzsche 2001a, 259), morality has subordinated us to its ultimately arbitrary but perverse strictures, preventing humanity from realising its *'highest potential and splendour'* (Nietzsche 2006, 6). Instead of being blond beasts of prey, we have been tamed to the level of a household pet (Nietzsche 2006, 11), and from that, we follow the morality of the herd, merely pacified, ineffective animals (2001a, 202).

However, morality and values themselves have no *true* content. Nothing gives them their authority other than people's acquiescence to them. Nietzsche sees that humanity has acquiesced to Christian morality, which emphasises weakness and compassion over strength. Its strictures have distorted the will into a futile battle to negate itself. Humanity complies through the twisting of the animal bad conscience (about which Nietzsche is intrigued) into sin and debt (against which Nietzsche is polemic). Our feelings of guilt and debt have been internalised as owed to God, to whom we owe the greatest debt. We expend our lives in suffering in order to repay that unpayable debt. The account of sin is thus 'the most dangerous and disastrous trick of religious interpretation' (2001a, 20). Whilst the religious consciousness is Nietzsche's primary target, any philosophy of improvement and enlightenment, from the Socratic to the scientific, is an ascetic ideal and a misunderstanding (1990, 44).

This mis-living of life comes from the use of sin and the concepts associated with it. God as divine Judge, transcendence, eternity, and hell are manifestations of the twisted will to power of the priestly class. Themselves weak, they fear the strong and have distorted their weakness into power over the strong, undergirded and justified by the idea of God. Therefore, when Nietzsche calls for the eradication of the concept of God and its attendant effects, he is realistic about what that would entail: the complete dissolution of a worldview and its values.

To move to *The Gay Science,* whilst this is welcome and necessary, it is a traumatic event with consequences that people are loathe to engage with. So the shadow of God persists: he comments that 'after Buddha was dead, they still showed his shadow in a cave for centuries – a tremendous, gruesome shadow.

God is dead; but given the way people are, there may still for millennia be caves in which they show his shadow. And we – we must still defeat his shadow as well!' (2001b, s.108). The madman of Nietzsche's parable knows that God is dead and that we have killed him. But he comes to realise that his audience continue as they were, unaware that they have 'unchained this earth from its sun' that they are 'plunging continually' and 'straying, as though through an infinite nothing' (2001b, s.125).

With the death of God comes the death of all values: a nihilism.[18] To those who are naturally strong, they are able to create their own world and values from this void. They engage in the transvaluation of all values. As he allegorises it in the 'Three Metamorphoses' of *Thus Spake Zarathustra*, having been the camel, the beast of burden, we come to destroy the great dragon 'thou shalt' with the leonine 'I will'. From that, we become the child whose innocence and forget-fulness bring about the new beginning, the 'sacred Yes' needed for the spirit to 'now will *its own* will' and 'win *its own world*' (1969, 55).

Although Nietzsche focuses less on despair and anxiety, his focus on the individual, his account of morality, and the transvaluation of values are crucial to existentialism, particularly to atheistic instantiations. Furthermore, he is attentive to the importance and role of God as a psychological guarantee and horizon, even in rejecting God in his own account of authentic, free, individual existence.[19] Nietzsche is in his own way an optimist, but even in his positive programme for human existence, there is an ambiguity that will persist in existentialism proper.

2.5 Martin Heidegger (1889–1976)

Heidegger is another figure often listed as an existentialist despite his rejection of Sartre's slogan that 'existence precedes essence'. In his *Letter on Humanism*, he dismisses it as merely the reversal of the metaphysical statement that essence gives rise to existence; hence, it 'remains a metaphysical statement' (Heidegger 1977, 250). Instead, Heidegger's quintessential, anti-metaphysical statement is that the essence of Dasein lies in its existence. If Heidegger does not mean what

---

[18] In the posthumously published *Will to Power*, he defines nihilism as 'that the highest values devaluate themselves. The aim is lacking; "why?" finds no answer' (Nietzsche 1968, 9).

[19] Cavell notes this ambiguity that 'you may battle against the Christian's self-understanding from within Christianity, as Kierkegaard declares, or from beyond Christianity, as Nietzsche declares. In both cases, you are embattled because you find the words of the Christian to be the right words. It is the way he means them that is empty or enfeebling. Christianity appears in Nietzsche not so much as the reverse of the truth but as the truth in foul disguise. In particular, the problem seems to be that human action is everywhere disguised as human suffering: this is what acceptance of the Will to Power is to overcome' (Cavell 1979, 352).

Sartre ascribes to him and, in doing so, rejects the label of existentialism, then what exactly does Heidegger mean by this?

We find the answer in Heidegger's 1927 work *Being and Time*. Here, Heidegger espouses a new methodology for detailing being. He starts neither from metaphysical first principles nor from the phenomenological method of his teacher Husserl[20] but from one's being in the world. Focusing on this individual experience, being is always that of a particular entity. It is not something beyond the human, as it had been seen by '"metaphysics" and transcendental philosophy of modern times' (Heidegger 1962, 22[43]). Nothing underlies our existence, and there is nothing beyond it to sleuth out. Instead, we are thrown into the world, and our *Dasein*, our own existing being, must find its own way through it.

It is in this thrownness that we are subject to what Heidegger terms 'fallenness'. Instead of choosing our own existence, we surrender the choice to others within the world. We engage in idle talk; 'the possibility of understanding everything without previously making the thing one's own' (1962, 169[213]). Then we fall: distracted by the 'they', the mass, we are carried along by the world, relinquishing our own choices. In this passivity, 'Dasein lets itself be carried along [mitnehmen] solely by the looks of the world; in this kind of Being, it concerns itself with becoming rid of itself as Being-in-the-world and rid of its Being alongside that which, in the closest everyday manner, is ready-to-hand' (1962, 172[216]).

This alienation of the self from itself closes off Dasein from the possibility of authenticity, forcing it into inauthenticity. The self then becomes the they-self; it falls. This is the risk of our being with others in the world. Dasein does not want to have authenticity because it is easier to follow the 'they'. Yet, even in our adoption of the 'they', we are not immune from anxiety, which overtakes us and renders the world in which we find ourselves *unheimlich*. This anxiety, however, is the possibility of our authentic existence: it is the experience of our freedom. In contrast, fallenness and inauthenticity are our evasion of the truth of our ownmost possibility, our death, and the commensurate ending of our possibilities.

Whilst the closing down of possibilities evokes anxiety and angst, death is also the possibility of our authenticity. Facing up to death, which is our own individual possibility, and being resolute in the face of it; making our choices in the knowledge and acceptance of it allows the self, 'in this individualisation of

---

[20] Heidegger differentiates his method from the more epistemological concerns of Husserl. For Heidegger, 'ontology and phenomenology are not two distinct philosophical disciplines among others ... philosophy is universal phenomenological ontology, and takes it departure from the hermeneutic of Dasein, which, as an analytic of *existence*, has made fast the guiding-line for all philosophical inquiry at the point where it *arises* and to which it *returns*' (1962, 38[62]).

itself, to become certain of the totality of its potentiality-for-Being' (266[310]). Heidegger's process of coming to authentic existence and the focus on the individual echoes Augustine and Kierkegaard's account of existence, although he substitutes death for the divine. Heidegger's turn away from prior under-standings of being involves seeing the call towards authenticity as coming not from God but from being itself. We must orient ourselves towards our ownmost possibility: our own death, rather than God.

The idea of God in fact prevents us from coming to authentic existence, from asking the question of what our being is. It gives us an answer before we are able to even pose the question. This is somewhat ironic considering Heidegger's descriptions of human existence draw from the presentations of Augustine, Luther, and Kierkegaard. This inheritance is underscored in his 1920 lecture series *The Phenomenology of Religious Life*. Heidegger's philosophy has a fraught relationship with Christian accounts of existence. He writes in the late 1930s that 'my entire path so far has been accompanied by a silent engage-ment with Christianity', although whether he achieves his 'painful emancipa-tion from it' (Heidegger 2006, 415) is contestable. Indeed, Heidegger's vision of existence proved to be fertile ground for varied theological interpreters.

It is not just Heidegger's vision of existence that proved of interest. His resistance to the strictures of metaphysics was also seen as theologically productive. His 1945 essay 'On Nietzsche's Word "God is Dead"' argues that seeing God as the ground of being or the *causa sui* does not merely lead humans to forget being, but it is also 'the ultimate blow against God and against the suprasensory world'. God, as the first of beings, 'is degraded to the highest value' (Heidegger 1977, 105). Heidegger's response is not to hail the death of God à la Nietzsche, as that leads to an approach where the individual, as subject, imposes itself on the world.[21] Instead, in the essay 'The Onto-Theological Constitution of Metaphysics', Heidegger calls for an almost mystical, apophatic relation, where this 'god-less thinking, which must abandon the god of philoso-phy, god as *causa sui*, is thus perhaps closer to the divine God' (Heidegger 1969, 72). After all, one can 'neither pray nor sacrifice to this god. Before the *causa sui*, man can neither fall to his knees in awe nor can he play music and dance before this god' (Heidegger 1969).

Heidegger's philosophy, with its account of anxious, searching existence hemmed in by time and death, haunted by the nothingness that gives rise to the world, has an Augustinian tenor. His account of authentic existence moves the responsibility for certainty and resoluteness to the individual alone. We move from the passivity of Pascal and the rest of Augustine to the repetition of

---

[21] 'The uprising of man into subjectivity transforms that which is into object' (1977, 107).

authentic existence alongside a Kierkegaardian suspension, albeit over nothing-ness rather than 70,000 fathoms. In his later thought, Heidegger will speak more of human receptivity, moving from this constant, choosing authenticity to a more passive, poetic position where only a god can save us. However, he has paved the way for a more godless understanding of existence, characterised by finitude, anxiety, despair, and the individual choice, where one cannot stabilise or base existence in the being of God, nor find rest and stability in human existence.

2.6 Karl Jaspers (1883–1969)

Karl Jaspers's *Existenzphilosophie* contains an attentiveness to God that led the psychiatrist turned philosopher to be labelled as a Catholic existentialist by Sartre, despite him not being Catholic. And whilst Jaspers's three-volume *Philosophie* is oriented towards the figure of God and the attendant concept of oneness, he argues that that stance is philosophical rather than religious. In doing so, Jaspers will deliberately resist the rest and the stability granted to the individual in Augustine, Pascal, and even Kierkegaard.

In the 1955 epilogue to the 3rd German edition of *Existenz*, Jaspers comments that he thought he had invented the term 'existentialism' when he was writing *Von der Wahrheit* just before and during World War II, only to find post-1945 that the term had turned up in France, attached to a different philosophy. Although that philosophy arose from similar sources, Jaspers distances himself from it, remarking that this kind of existentialism was not one he either antici-pated or sought to pursue.

Jaspers is heavily influenced by Kierkegaard, Kant, and Nietzsche. One way of describing Jaspers's *Existenzphilosophie* is that it effectively transposes the Kierkegaardian leap. Rather than being from one's finite situatedness to the infinite, it is a psychological movement of transcendence from particular situ-ations called boundary or limit situations (*Grenzsituationen*). To make this move is to exist in a certain way: philosophy, as a particular *way* of existing, is to transcend. It is an activity, a posture towards the world that is fundamen-tally concerned with the individual and their search for meaning in the situations in which we find ourselves.

In Jaspers's work, he sees that we exist as fundamentally self-reflective consciousnesses that are oriented in a world that we cannot become one with nor separate from: again there is the sense that the self is not reconcilable. In this world, we find ourselves in situations, some of which are *Grenzsituationen*. These include guilt, struggle, suffering, and death. We cannot exist without these boundary situations: life is never free from suffering or feelings of guilt, and we cannot escape death. They give rise to anxiety and feelings of despair and dread, and we are faced with a choice in relation to these situations.

That choice is to take a decisive leap or to refrain from doing so. Jaspers sees we cannot just remain as we are, merely existing, for 'to realise myself, I leave the possibilities behind. From the emptiness of the rich world I step into the abundance of a world that is poor compared with the other, but becomes real and is sustained by self-being' (Jaspers 1970, 161). We either transcend to become ourselves or we do not, and he distinguishes *Dasein*, what he terms mere 'existence', from Existenz. *Dasein* is to be closed off and without transcendence, to descend, whereas in Existenz we become truly ourselves. We are torn between two ways of existing; in familiar language, he writes that '*man* is the nothingness of a speck of dust in the limitless universe – and he is a creature of a depth capable of recognising the universe and of encompassing it within itself. He is both, between both' (Jaspers 1971a, 72).

We *must* make a choice as we are caught between the world and transcendence. We do not exist without the world, but we cannot become ourselves without transcendence. We have to continually choose to become ourselves. Although we seek unity, oneness, and rest, if we are to live authentically we cannot have that. Nor can we ignore it as we are *related* to oneness: 'Existenz feels dependent upon a transcendence that has willed what seems to be the utmost possibility: a free, self-originating being' (1970, 46). Yet, despite our relation to oneness, to that 'wholly Other that makes it aware of being by itself alone' (1970, 4), Existenz cannot be or become a certainty. Instead, the 'touchstone of any philosophy of Existenz' is its inconclusiveness (Jaspers 1969, 67).

Whilst Jaspers's language of the leap is more everyday, it is still used in relation to God, albeit a hidden one. Our relation to God cannot come at the expense of the inconclusiveness and the activity of philosophising. The necessarily hidden deity must be searched for and related to. God's concealment 'requires the freedom of Existenz as a condition of all truth in time. Existenz attains itself in the darkness of transcendence without receiving objectively certain demands and answers from transcendence' (1970, 280). God remains hidden if we are to be free, and thus, we must have faith. The core of our worldview *is* faith, but faith is not rest or stability; it is a constant tension between itself and unbelief.

Hence, Jaspers is critical of mystics, who seek to remove themselves from time and find absoluteness outside of it. Instead, our existence should be philosophical, rather than mystical or religious. Philosophy remains contrary to revelation, authority, and timelessness. Philosophy is a form of faith, but one without definite content as the One 'can never be definitively stated. Existenz will not find its reality in this or that sphere; it will serve its one God, knowing him only in doing what it must do, not otherwise' (1969, 268). Jaspers sees that whilst 'I shall never know what God is, what makes me sure of him is what I am' (1971b, 108). The figure of God is more a horizon that enables Existenz, one that we must continuously authentically exist in relation to.

The focus on the individual in Jaspers is such that 'each Existenz is always only itself, not a picture for others' (1970, 382). Each individual must make these choices for themselves. Similarly, the God that we relate to is not some objective reality in which we all come to share and rest, instead 'God is always God for the individual Existenz alone' (1969, 265). This is the structure and pattern of our existence: unable to survey the whole or attain oneness, we seek it, in the encompassing, the horizon in which we live which 'forces us to give up any final rest' (1955, 52). Yet we can find in relation to that horizon our Existenz, and be the individual that comprehends themselves standing both before transcendence and nothingness, in the face of which 'I am what I can be *through myself alone*' (1971a, 28). Jaspers's thought needs to relate to God for Existenz to be possible through the movement of transcendence. However, that relationship provides no rest or certainty.

2.7 Conclusion

To conclude this section, we can observe similarities but also shifts in these proto-existentialists. There is a continuous engagement with monotheism in these proto-existentialists, but the figure of God and what that figure guarantees shifts: from God acting as an end or guiding the purpose of human existence, towards a restlessness that cannot or should not be satisfied. The diagnoses of human existence and the human condition tend to reoccur in each thinker, finding anxiety and despair in the individual and their response to the world, in the face of its demands and distractions, or in relation to the transcendent and its disjunction and impossibility in the face of human existence. Turning now to atheistic existentialism proper, I will argue that not only do the above diagnoses of human existence persist, but the conceptions of God do as well. God not only haunts existentialism proper but also appears clearly within it: as a challenge and a solution.

3 Survivors of the Death of God

Having explored the inheritance of existentialism, we come now to existentialism proper: how it came to be and how best to define it. The second question remains elusive as existentialism's heyday was cultural as well as philosophical. The popular vision of existentialism, shaped by Sartre and Beauvoir's post–World War II work, was communicated in lectures, articles, novels, and plays.[22] The latter mediums often had more impact than the former, and although this aided the communication of ideas, it is harder to draw philosophical boundaries and espouse philosophical doctrines in novels and plays without them ceasing to be literature and being didactic.

New work on the emergence of Sartre and Beauvoir's brand of existentialism has contested the usual genealogy that locates existentialism's origin in Sartre's reception of Husserl and Heidegger's phenomenology through Raymond Aron, alongside Sartre's reading of Heidegger's *Being and Time* as a prisoner of war (Crowell 2020). These newer readings focus more on the philosophical atmosphere 'at home'. Whilst not disavowing the importance of Husserl and Heidegger, they make the point that a number of the spurs for existentialism proper came from ideas already percolating within France. These spurs include the influence of French Augustinianism and the interwar reception of Nietzsche, Kierkegaard, and Jaspers, aided by the work of Jean Wahl.[23] The philosophy of Husserl and Heidegger, which permeated French philosophy most thoroughly in the 1920s, is certainly influential, but if their thought sparked what became known as existentialism, the fire had long been banked.

Alongside this work on the intellectual and cultural atmosphere around the birth of existentialism proper have come new explorations of how best to define existentialism. Jonathan Webber has argued that existentialism should be aligned to the definition that Sartre and Beauvoir agreed on by 1952, as 'the ethical theory that we ought to treat the freedom at the core of human existence as intrinsically valuable and the foundation of all other values' (Webber 2018, 1–2). Classical existentialism, as he defines it, is founded in Sartre's comment that 'existence precedes essence' and its inherent denial of human nature even whilst it details the human condition. The more detailed definition is that 'existentialism is defined by the idea that existence precedes essence, the idea that we have the freedom over the values that organise our experience and so shape our behaviour' (Webber 2018, 6). This allows him to read existentialist texts as espousing an optimistic, eudaimonistic vision, and despite his desire to return to an original definition, what he reads into the texts and thinkers serves perhaps another vision.

Sartre and Beauvoir's reification of the definition in the latter half of the 1940s came from their own attempts to take control of existentialism in the popular imagination. Their efforts to move away from the perception of

---

[22] Malpas (2012) and Schacht (2012) suggest that existentialism should be restricted to Sartre's definitions.

[23] For the importance of French Augustinianism on the development of existentialism, see Kirkpatrick 2017; for the reception of Nietzsche and Kierkegaard, see Descombes 1991, 101; Teboul 2005, 315.

the movement as outré and pessimistic met with varying success. Despite their disdain for the demand that existentialism could be expressed as a slogan, 'existence precedes essence' became the unofficial slogan of existentialism. Yet this slogan can be helpful, as I see it encapsulates the foundational ontology of existentialism proper. It is further a useful touchstone for the difficulties they experienced in setting forth existentialist ethics, coalescing as they must around the limitation and implications of this statement. Despite Sartre's later ambivalence, it is helpful to return to Sartre's 1945 'Existentialism Is a Humanism' to explore how this seminal definition of existentialism came to be.

Sartre comes to this lecture aiming to disprove certain negative judgements about existentialism: that it is quietist in the face of despair, dwells on what is sordid in human nature, is fundamentally based on individual subjectivity, and does away with morality. Sartre instead argues that despite the bleak vision of existence found in *Being and Nothingness*, existentialism presents a positive vision of human existence. The slogan that existence precedes essence is pivotal to many of the claims that Sartre wants to make as it rejects any basis for human existence that is not found in human freedom. This excludes Christianity, for in that ontological vision, God is a supernatural artisan who 'makes man according to a procedure and a conception, exactly as the artisan fashions a paper knife, following a definition and a formula'. Therefore, each individual human existence is not freely chosen but is instead a realisation of a 'certain conception which dwells in the divine understanding' (Sartre 1948, 27). Existentialism is defined in explicit contrast to God: if there is no given essence, then man is 'nothing else but that which he makes of himself' (28). This is liberating but also the cause of despair and anxiety. For now, there is nothing that makes our actions right or wrong, nor anything that can support or justify the choices we make. With a nod to Dostoevsky's *Brothers Karamazov*, he remarks that 'everything is indeed permitted if God does not exist, and man is in consequence forlorn, for he cannot find anything to depend upon either within or outside himself' (34).

In the same year, Simone de Beauvoir wrote the article 'Existentialism and Popular Wisdom'. In this text, she engages both with how existentialism is misrepresented in popular wisdom and how it coheres with and challenges it. She sees existentialism as presenting an honest account of life: it does not seek to elide the despair and anxiety in life by covering it up with narratives and stories and external justifications. It accepts that we are both engaged with the world but also seek to transcend our situations and that 'I exist as an authentic subject, in a constantly renewed upspringing that is opposed to the fixed reality of things. I throw myself without help and without guidance into a world where I am not installed ahead of time waiting for myself' (Beauvoir 2004[1945],

212). Although we are nothing, as we have no human nature and no known end, our freedom means that we are able to, and must, want our own existence. As she writes in 1947's 'What is Existentialism?' 'the task of man is one: to fashion the world by giving it a meaning. This meaning is not given ahead of time, just as the existence of each man is not justified ahead of time either' (2004[1947], 325). This comes with a rejection of the divine, for if there is a God, then our values are given to us, not freely chosen.

In these definitional texts, there exists a clear negative definition of existentialism, formed in contrast to the figure of God granting essence and values. Yet the engagement with God in the work of Sartre and Beauvoir is more complex than this. Although their *oeuvre* develops in different directions, the following pieces are foundational to existentialism proper and engage with the claim that existence precedes essence. I will explore how in these texts they truly engage with God, the implications of monotheism in their thought, and how the rejection is not as straightforward as the existentialist offensive claims. I then turn to the thought of Albert Camus, who has both a more ambiguous position on God and on human nature. His status as an existentialist is also contested as he holds that humanity has a nature or essence. Yet that ambiguity allows him more space in affirming a transcendence that is not fundamentally useless, although it is fundamentally not existentialist.

3.1 Jean-Paul Sartre (1905–1980): A Useless Passion

What is it like to *exist*? This is the central concern of *La Nausée* (1938), the philosophical and deeply phenomenological novel with which Sartre rose to prominence. Presented as the recovered diary of one Antoine Roquentin, it details his encounters with existence that take the form of intense, dizzying nausea sparked by the alienness of various objects. This comes to a head in an encounter with a chestnut tree at which he realises the fundamental absurdity of the world and its lack of meaning. Existence, if it is anything, is *de trop*. Sartre leaves us with a perverse Cartesianism, in which 'I exist – the world exists – and I know that the world exists. That's all' (Sartre 1938, 156). Nothing gives the world or our existence meaning: not God, not the brotherhood of all humanity, not love and companionship. Existence just is, nothing more, nothing less.

La Nausée was written alongside a more explicit work of philosophical phenomenology, 1936's *The Transcendence of the Ego*. Here, he argues contra Husserl that the self, our ego, is not something given to us but an object that we have to create and sustain by 'a sort of preserving spontaneity' (Sartre 1960, 78). The self is a 'perpetually elusive mirage', one we are always in the process of creating. We make ourselves through the act and movement of transcendence and the exercise of our freedom. It is here that we also find the theological language that Sartre attributes to the human subject: where 'each instant of our conscious life reveals to us a creation *ex nihilo*. Not a new *arrangement*, but a new existence' (98–99). We also have here the glimmers of what is later termed bad faith (*mauvaise foi)* in *Being and Nothingness* when Sartre muses that 'perhaps the essential role of the ego is to mask from consciousness its very spontaneity' (100).

Sartre's preoccupation with God and creation even as he dismisses God's existence and the effects thereof has been long noted. Desan writes that 'more than any other philosopher he has emphasised the extreme need of the absolute, without, however, conceding the existence of an Absolute Being as a remedy to this obsession' (Desan 1954, 179). Sartre himself alludes to this, commenting in a 1943 review of George Bataille's *Inner Experience* that Bataille is a survivor of the death of God and that the entire age is marked by it. Sartre writes 'God is dead ... he used to speak to us and he has fallen silent, we now touch only his corpse' (Sartre 2010, 234). This sense of being marked by God even more in the absence than in God's existence pervades Sartre's *Being and Nothingness*, published in the same year, which advances a phenomenological account of being through vivid examples drawn from various fraught interpersonal relationships.

Being and Nothingness's analysis is dependent on a particular vision of God: as a stable, constant, and fully realised being. Human freedom is, as in Descartes, akin to the freedom of God but ever frustrated by the lack in our being. Yet this freedom and this being do not have its source, as Descartes's did, in God. Instead, being is uncreated, 'without reason for being, without any connection with another being', it is excessive, superfluous, '*de trop* for eternity' (Sartre 1992, 29).

Human being is composed of facticity (our physical, embodied existence and the situation in which we find ourselves) and nothingness (our consciousness, characterised by its freedom and desire to transcend). Our Being is further differentiated into the incompatible and irreconcilable states of being-in-itself, for-itself, and for-others. Being-in-itself is self-identical, inert, and passive, whereas being-for-itself is lack and freedom and cannot be self-identical and inert the way an apple, lacking consciousness, is. That nothingness is at the heart of our being, and we are suspended in our freedom such that there is 'no difference between the being of man and his *being-free*' (Sartre 1992, 25). This freedom is the reason for the anguish that plagues existence, as it is in anguish that 'freedom is, in its being, in question for itself' (Sartre 1992, 29).

Nothingness, freedom, and anguish are inextricably bound up with each other; they are the heart of the relation between our present and future being, our motives and our acts. We can never achieve wholeness, unity, or rest in our existence, but we try to achieve this, seeking some kind of oneness or looking for something external to paper over this gap. This deception is bad faith, the negation of the self from the self, the rearranging of our perception of reality to convince ourselves that we have a particular end.

This can be sought in ourselves, in others, or in a role, as shown his famous discussions of a woman on a date and the waiter. The woman continues in her sustained ignorance of her companion's intentions even when he takes her hand. She lets it instead rest as an indifferent object, neither consenting nor resisting, delaying the moment when she must make a choice, refusing to accept the truth. The waiter plays his role too eagerly, exaggerating his behaviour, playing the role of someone playing at *being* a waiter in a café. This acting betrays that he is consciously deceiving himself.

The discussion of bad faith underscores the preoccupation with monotheism and its effects. Sartre writes that the problem with bad faith is not necessarily that it has the wrong ends but that it is *faith*. Belief, where being adheres to something that is either not given or given indistinctly, is for Sartre epistemologically and ontologically an impossibility. If we believe, we know that we believe, for 'to know that one believes is no longer to believe'. Therefore, 'to believe is not-to-believe' (Sartre 1992, 68).

The previous discussion and examples raise the question of whether there can be a way of existing in good faith. However, in an oft-discussed note, Sartre appears to disavow the possibility of any faith being good or having a good end. Good faith, he notes, would be an ideal of being-in-itself, the possibility of authenticity. Good faith would be able to be re-apprehended by bad faith and thus slide 'to the very origin of the project of good faith'. We may not escape bad faith, but there would be the possibility of 'a self-recovery of being which was previously corrupted'. This self-recovery would be authenticity, but Sartre remarks that 'has no place here' (Sartre 1992, 70n9). It is here we first get language pertaining to the idea of a fall and an ideal being. In the discussion here, the ontological consequences of the absence of God are also the absence of good faith or authentic existence.

This comes out more clearly in part II, where Sartre's account of being navigates what our existence is like and what we want but can never be: like God, stable and at rest. As being that is in-itself but then also for-itself, we are a lack: our facticity, our givenness, and our situation are at odds with our transcendence, nothingness, and freedom. We can decide what we make of our facticity, but we cannot ground ourselves, even though we have the desire to, and our desire is also a lack. Our desire to be as God is impossible as even the idea of God is impossible. For if God is conceived as self-grounding, as *causa sui*, this is contradictory. The 'act of causation by which God is *causa sui* is a nihilating act like every recovery of the self by the self, to same degree that the original relation of necessity is a return to *self*, a reflexivity' (Sartre 1992, 80–81). Thus, if God exists, God would be ontologically contingent and could not be God.

Yet this knowledge does not prevent us from desiring that stability and oneness. Sartre now describes existence in a twist on Descartes's fourth meditation. There, positioned between being and nothingness, our imperfect being attested to the perfect being as we know our imperfection only in relation to the innate idea of perfection in God. In Sartre, our being retains this structure and this impetus to surpass ourselves, but 'the being toward which human reality surpasses itself is not a transcendent God; it is at the heart of human reality; it is only human reality itself as totality' (Sartre 1992, 89). We reach only towards the world and its imperfections, despite being structured such that we are haunted by the idea of God, 'this perpetually absent being which haunts the for-itself is itself fixed in the in-itself' (Sartre 1992, 90).

Thus, Sartre psychologizes the Cartesian structure of existence, and we hypostasise this impossible being as transcendence beyond the world, giving it the name of God. Whether or not God is actual is irrelevant, it is part of our make-up. We still relate to God, and

> human reality is suffering because it rises in being as perpetually haunted by a totality which it is without being able to be it. Precisely because it could not attain the in-itself without losing itself as for-itself. Human reality therefore is by nature an unhappy consciousness with no possibility of surpassing its unhappy state. (Sartre 1992, 90)

We find no rest when it comes to our relations to others either. Our being-for-others is characterised by shame, framed again with theological language and the idea of a fall. Sartre illustrates this shame through the example of a voyeur looking through a keyhole. Upon hearing footsteps, the voyeur feels himself subject to the look, *le regard*, even though there may be no one there. He then feels shame because his being has been observed, and in that instant he realises he has become an object for another even as he was making others an object for himself.

In relating to others as objects, we are caught in a continuous whorl of objectifying from which we cannot escape. The existence of the Other is then our 'original fall' (Sartre 1992, 263). The shame that results is not because of our actions before or towards the other, but 'simply that I have "fallen" into the world in the midst of things and that I need the mediation of the Other in order to be what I am' (Sartre 1992, 288–289). This results in the dynamic that leads the character Garcin in the play *Huis Clos* to conclude that hell is other people ('L'enfer . . . c'est les autres!'). Again, God and transcendence are seen to be the non-existent end of an unfulfillable desire: to have our actions externally justified and to be fully known as a subject by a subject, for our totality to be apprehended (Sartre 1992, 302).

Therefore, not only is our being-in-itself and being-for-itself haunted by the impossible God, but our being-for-others is also similarly haunted (Sartre 1992, 365). We are hemmed in by the contradictory ideals of God and love. We remain, in ourselves and in relation to others 'separated by an insurmountable nothingness'. Like our own being, 'the problem of my being-for-others remains therefore without solution' (Sartre 1992, 376). We are not only *de trop* in our own individuality but also *de trop* in relation to others. It is from this that guilt and sin are derived. We are ashamed and guilty before the Other, alienated and fallen, and even in our turning towards the other 'by the very fact of my own self-assertion I constitute him as an object and as an instrument, and I cause him to experience that same alienation which he must now assume'. Original sin is 'my upsurge in a world where there are others; and whatever may be my further relations with others, these relations will be only variations on the original theme of my guilt' (Sartre 1992, 410). We cannot constitute or ground ourselves, nor ground or constitute ourselves on another, and whilst our nature is the exercise of our freedom, the unpredictable freedom of another is the limit of ours (Sartre 1992, 262).

In the final part of *Being and Nothingness*, the relationship of the human mind and psyche to God is further delineated. Here, having, being, and doing are the cardinal categories of human reality under which human conduct is subsumed. Again, Sartre stresses how God would limit us, as if God gave us ends, we would be passive, accepting rather than choosing. The freedom that is ours has 'nothing to do with an essence or with a property of a being which would be engendered conjointly with an idea' (Sartre 1992, 444). In this particular formulation of existence preceding essence, freedom is inseparable from existence and cannot be reconciled with essence.

It is also here that Sartre underscores both humanity's desire to be God and God as humanity's ideal. God, that being that is a totality, the 'in-itself-for-itself', is what humanity desires and 'thus the best way to conceive of the fundamental project of human reality is to say that man is the being whose project is to be God'. Our mix of being and nothingness, of facticity and freedom reaches towards the being of God, hence 'man is fundamentally the desire to be God' (Sartre 1992, 566). Not only is our desire for God in being, but we also wish to be like God in possessing and having, to be that being whose 'possession is in its own creation' (Sartre 1992, 592).

Indeed, God appears to be not merely an impossible desire but the necessary support for Sartre's vision. Sartre writes that 'my freedom is a choice of being God and all my acts, all my projects translate this choice and reflect it in a thousand and one ways, for there is an infinity of ways of being and of ways of having' (Sartre 1992, 599). Each human reality, in the end, seeks to metamorphose itself into God, that in-itself-for-itself, to be the *ens causa sui*. Thus, Sartre writes that 'the passion of man is the reverse of that of Christ, for man loses himself as man in order that God may be born. But the idea of God is contradictory and we lose ourselves in vain. Man is a useless passion' (Sartre 1992, 615).

Reading *Being and Nothingness*, it is as if everyone and everything wants to be God, yet nothing can be God, not even God. At times, God acts as a psychological necessity, with Sartre writing that 'man makes himself man in order to be God' (Sartre 1992, 626). Whilst we cannot be the ideal, we have no choice but to attempt the ideal. Nevertheless, we still end up in our fraught, inauthentic, haunted individual being, haunted by wholeness, struggling with our impossible demand for love, justification, fullness, and rest.

Even authenticity, the achievable ideal and aim of some proto-existentialists, is discounted here as having no place. Whilst Webber sees that bad faith is to have the desire to be God as our fundamental project (Webber 2009, 109), it appears more as our inescapable drive. Even accepting it as our drive cannot stop it from taking place. Bad faith is simply the nature of our existence, as it is not merely the denial of our freedom and transcendence. We can never not desire to be God but we also can never authentically choose to be or not to be God. Both being and love are unrealisable ideals and useless passions, but the desire for them is the condition of our existence.

There is, however, perhaps some ambiguity in Sartre concerning the end of this desire. Do we desire God or desire to be God? Is our desire for fullness and rest, or do we want power and control? In Sartre, this is often elided, and yet the *kind* of freedom he speaks of is divine. In Sartre, the concept of God is necessary for human existence, in order to explain *what* our freedom is. This is expressed in Sartre's 1943 play, *The Flies*, his revisioning of Elektra. When Orestes discovers his radical freedom in the actual face of Zeus, he discovers freedom that makes the gods 'powerless against him' (Sartre 1976, 102). It is a freedom that crashes down on him, that sweeps him off his feet, emptying the heavens such that there is 'no right or wrong, nor anyone to give me orders' (118). Again, the radically free human and the divine are not so different, as Orestes reflects to Zeus that 'you are God and I am free; each of us is alone and our anguish is akin'

(119). Yet despite Sartre's efforts to make Orestes into a revaluing Nietzschean figure and his comment in *Being and Nothingness* that man seeks the reversal of Christ, Orestes ends up as a strangely Christlike figure, taking on the sin and guilt of those in Argos, freeing them from the curse they lived under.

The play is a helpful microcosm of Sartre's tangled relationship to monotheism and religion, and despite the implied polytheistic setting, the ontology is profoundly monotheistic. The problem of monotheism is the problem of passivity, of accepting our being from another as an absolute. The problem of passivity is also the source of our tension with the Other, this constant activity of self in choosing, asserting, and creating itself, thereby inhibiting any social relations that are true and any self-relation that could be authentic.

Yet Sartre's philosophy *needs* monotheism; it needs God. It needs God not just as a foil, or something to negatively define itself against, but also as something to support the positive claims it makes: about human existence and its drives and desires and about freedom and its potentiality, power, and possibility. I noted that Sartre modulates his account of freedom to be like Beauvoir's, and I will return to that shift in the conclusion. I turn now to the thought of Beauvoir, focusing in particular on the ethical vision she created from existentialism, and how she, in collaboration, conversation, and combat with Sartre, made something of existentialism herself.

3.2 Simone de Beauvoir (1908–1986): Sedimented Freedom and Dangerous Devotion

Simone de Beauvoir was perhaps initially more of a reluctant existentialist than Sartre, with whom she is inextricably associated. Like Sartre, she was initially known as a writer, coming to prominence with novels such as *L'Invitée* and *Les Mandarins*. She made her name not only with her joint work on the existentialist offensive with Sartre but with the seminal feminist text *The Second Sex*. She has therefore been seen either as a more cultural than philosophical accomplice of Sartre in existentialism or as concerned with a phenomenological and ethical approach to feminism.

This section will focus on two works in which she sought to negotiate an existentialist ethics. The first came about when she was asked by Jean Grenier to contribute an existentialist perspective to an anthology he was editing. Despite not seeing herself as an existentialist nor as necessarily able to contribute a philosophical text, she was encouraged by Sartre to accept. She decided to reflect on his account of being and freedom in dialogue with her own account of being situated in the world. Thus, 1944's *Pyrrhus and Cinéas* can be seen as the first explicit attempt at an existentialist ethics. She takes off where *Being and*

Nothingness ends, which notes that whilst ethics were a concern, they would be addressed in a 'later work'.

Pyrrhus and Cinéas is broad in its scope, taking its direction from a conversation between Pyrrhus, the fourth century BC king of Epirus, and his advisor, Cineas. Discussing Pyrrhus's plans to conquer the world and then rest (a famously qualified success), Cineas asks, why not rest now? What difference would it make (2004[1944], 90)? This becomes the question of all humans and their projects: why *are* our projects and what is their use? After all, they are limited, and limits can always be met, expanded, and overridden. The text is then framed by the command of Christ to love your neighbour and Voltaire's remark in *Candide* that we must cultivate our garden. This then raises the attendant questions of who is your neighbour and what is your garden.

The absence of God in Beauvoir's scheme gives this question greater gravity for nothing is given. I can only recognise my being as mine where it is engaged. I can only determine my neighbour by creating the 'tie that unites me to the other' (2004[1944], 93); only I can determine the location and limits of my garden (2004[1944], 95). Beauvoir takes Sartre's account of the self as transcendence, a project of the self, but seeks to create a relationship to the other that is not solipsism and shame. She starts not from the nothingness of our being, but instead from our situatedness. The drive and impulse we have is to navigate our situatedness and decide the place we occupy in the world, for we 'can never withdraw from it' (2004[1944], 100).

Thus, Beauvoir reconfigures the meaning of the limits on our freedom. Our freedom is tempered in relation to another, but the other is not inherently hostile. They do not necessarily steal our being; instead, we need others in order for our existence to become 'founded and necessary' (2004[1944], 129). Our being, and our projects, gradually become sedimented by our choices and commitments.[24] She distinguishes here between the inner, absolute freedom of ourselves and others and our situations. We cannot control the inner freedom, but we can control the situations of others. My situation facing others entails that my freedom has a responsibility: we are free, thrown into the world amongst other, foreign freedoms.

We need these other, foreign freedoms because 'once I have surpassed my own goals, my actions will fall back on themselves, inert and useless, if they

---

[24] Sedimentation comes from Maurice Merleau-Ponty's *Phenomenology of Perception* (1945) and is the process of our taking on information about our situation as river accumulates sediment. Our actions are then informed by the bedrock built up through this sedimentation. Beauvoir's account of sedimentation is most fully explored in *The Second Sex*, but in these earlier works, there is the sense in how our projects become situated such that our actions are influenced by that.

have not been carried off toward a new future by new projects' (2004[1944], 135). Freedom now takes on a different role: it is the only reality that cannot be transcended, and it comes with a duty towards others, to achieve being, not egoism, to want the other 'to recognise my actions as valid and to make them into his good by taking them up in his name toward the future' (2004[1944], 136). The freedom of the other means that our proper relationship with them is to appeal to their freedom, rather than imposing our vision on them. We should therefore create situations in which they can 'accompany and surpass my transcendence' (2004[1944], 137). This paints a more positive picture of freedom than in *Being and Nothingness*; however, it is unclear how this new conception of situated freedom is supported or comes into being: it appears to just *be*.

Freedom therefore seems to take on status as an ideal; a value even. In *Being and Nothingness*, the ideal of God exists as a broken and impossible one. Beauvoir, like Sartre, rejects God in relation to being as God's existence entails a givenness and passivity in human existence. She comments that if God existed, it would be as a universal, which then would not be able to provide authenticity. Authenticity requires particularity and choice, rather than the silence of the universal. Her engagement with God here tends to take the form of throwaway, undeveloped comments, often echoing the critique of Sartre in *Being and Nothingness*. Her focus remains resolutely on the world and affirms our inability to get beyond it. The desire to escape the world and transcend ourselves in God is for her an evasion: for 'man cannot transcend himself in God if God is completely given' (2004[1944], 102). Instead, one 'must accomplish his redemption on earth' (2004[1944], 104). As we are creatures of this world, even God cannot provide us with an end that comes from outwith. Every attempt to connect with the infinite is futile as we are situated in a finite world and within humanity.

However, there is an interesting difference in how Beauvoir analyses both our desire for God and our desire to be God. The desire to be God is muted, and she spends more time on the dynamics of desiring to lose ourselves in devotion to God. In the desire to be God, she sees that someone who dreams of expanding themselves to infinity 'immediately loses himself. He loses himself in a dream because, in fact, he doesn't stop being there, attesting to his finite presence by his infinite projects' (2004[1944], 113). Whereas the desire to devote ourselves to God is to find our meaning by distracting ourselves from our existence, both in terms of recognising the other and in terms of losing ourselves to another. This desire is more natural to her and is replicated in our relationships with others.

In her rumination on devotion, she sees that to devote ourselves to another is to take them and their end as our own. This can be tyrannical, where in wanting the good of other, we in fact impose it on another and deny them their freedom. Devotion is an ontological error; it 'considers the other as an object carrying an emptiness in its heart that would be possible to fill' (2004[1944], 122). Our relation to others must navigate the Scylla and Charybdis of devotion and self-interest, which sees that the *néant* of the other can be filled by our action alone.

Yet, even in her rejection of the figure and concept of God for her ethical programme, she cannot stop considering that our desire is to be like God, to be a being 'capable of founding himself entirely by himself' that can 'also justify what I have founded by taking it as his own' (131). This ideal is impossible, and instead, freedom becomes the ideal that one should wish for oneself and for others. Is this perhaps just the exchange of one ideal for another? Freedom may not have the baggage that Beauvoir sees that God has, relationally, but as an ideal, God certainly has more positive content.

These themes and reflections continue in 1946's *The Ethics of Ambiguity*. Here, she is more certain of her existentialism and more confident in the ethical possibilities and mandates of that existentialism. She argues that existentialism is the only philosophy that can respond to Dostoevsky's claim that if God is dead, then everything is permitted. It does so through its understanding of freedom that, if it is properly enshrined and used, can be a challenge to oppressive political and social situations.

Yet we are not always aware of our freedom, and the role of the free individual is both to discover and author meaning in the world. Our existence is not absurd; it is ambiguous. In *Pyrrhus and Cinéas*, she pushed back on Camus's vision of human existence in *L'Étranger*, writing that the indifference of Meursault is not given. We are instead a 'spontaneity that desires, that loves, the wants, that acts', and to accept absurdity is to 'deny that I can even be given a meaning' (2004[1944], 93). In *The Ethics of Ambiguity*, she details a positive and productive vision of ambiguity, where to 'say that it is ambiguous is to assert that its meaning is never fixed, that it must be constantly won' (Beauvoir 2018, 139). Beauvoir states here that whilst *Being and Nothingness* cannot provide an ethics, she can provide one that does not succumb to the bleak vision of Sartre's or remain in solipsism. Due to the responsibility inherent in our freedom, where the source of all values is the freedom of humanity, the highest value and end of humanity is that 'to will oneself free is also to will others free' (Beauvoir 2018, 78).

Returning this analysis to the question and role of God, Beauvoir again rejects God as being able to ground our projects and our ideals. God is again this impossible synthesis of the for-itself and the in-itself, an existing being that one wishes would 'change his existence into being' (Beauvoir 2018, 13). God may be our impossible ontological ideal, as in Sartre, but Beauvoir spins that negative statement positively. She is open about the possibility and importance of failure as the progenitor of ambiguity. We may never succeed in discovering meaning, nor in being the author of meaning, as God is. But the future is open; it is ambiguous, not absurd, coloured with possibility and contoured by failure. The meaning that a God could give would be one that absolves us of responsibility for our successes as well as our failures, for 'a God can pardon, efface, and compensate. But if God does not exist, man's faults are inexpiable' (15). Instead, the individual is defined 'only by his relationship to the world and to other individuals, he exists only by transcending himself, and his freedom can be achieved only through the freedom of others' (169).

As Joseph Mahon notes, for someone who vehemently rejects God, Beauvoir certainly 'wrote an extraordinary amount about him' (2002, 165). I will return to the question of the effectiveness of her ethical vision, grounded on freedom, in relation to how Sartre takes it up in the conclusion. I close this section by noting that this account of freedom, which starts as absolute and becomes more sedimented, raises questions as to the suitability of freedom taking on a role that Sartre and Beauvoir originally castigate God as being: that which defines, limits, and is an end that we must work towards. Whilst I do not want to reduce Beauvoir's thought to Sartre's, she does modulate his freedom, and he comes to agree with this. Yet her modulations work with his ontological scheme, and it is not clear that his ontology modulates in response. Therefore, the ethical structure of atheistic, existentialist freedom may be built on a dangerous fault line.

3.3 Albert Camus (1931–1960): Benign Indifference and an Eternal Fall

Having explored the work of those who fully took on and sought to shape the term existentialism, we turn to someone who was somewhat of an outsider. A *pied noir*, Albert Camus was born and educated in Algeria and moved to Paris in the 1940s. There he finished his first cycle of works, the Sisyphus cycle (each cycle consisted of a novel, a play, and an essay). The novel in this cycle, *L'Étranger*, catapulted him to fame as well as into his association with existentialism. The accompanying essay, *The Myth of Sisyphus*, established him as a philosopher of the absurd, although Sartre, with whom he later fell out, commented that Camus was more a writer than a philosopher.[25] He thus came to the Parisian intellectual

---

[25] Camus himself reflects on this, writing 'why I am an artist and not a philosopher? Because I think according to words and not according to ideas' (Camus 1963, 113). The accompanying play is *Caligula*. I focus here on the novels and essays as they are more well-known.

and political scene outside of the elite circle of Parisian *lycées* and institutions such as the Sorbonne and the *École normale supérieure*

In those two works, Camus explores the alienation of the individual and the lack of meaning in existence. *L'Étranger* narrates the lack of attachment the protagonist Meursault has to the world, its demands, and relationships. When he shoots and kills the unnamed Arab, he finds it impossible to feel guilt as the legal and emotional fallout happens around him. The work ends with a brush with religion: as indifferent to God as he is to love, morality, and existence, Meursault is visited by the chaplain in his cell after his conviction and sentencing to death. Meursault again refuses to repent or see that he has committed an act that makes one guilty: whilst he has committed a criminal offence and been justly punished, his own relationship to that act is not one of guilt. Seeing all as condemned to death by virtue of being alive, Meursault expends, physically and emotionally, his last revolt against existence on the chaplain. After this, he finds himself purged: empty of evil and of hope, he opens himself up for the first time to the 'tendre indifférence du monde', feeling its fraternity with him and remembering his happiness. With this particular reconciliation and acceptance, he hopes at his death for there to be many spectators and for them to welcome him with cries of hatred.

In *The Myth of Sisyphus*, this reaction to the world is explored in philosophy and literature and analysed in relation to absurdity, meaning, and morality. Taking a particularly Nietzschean stance on values and their revaluation, with assists from Kierkegaard, Jaspers, Heidegger, Pascal, and a 'certain contemporary writer' on nausea, Camus notes that life is, normally, the unconscious, passive repetition of various habits. Yet, at times, one comes to realise 'the ridiculous nature of that habit, the absence of any profound reason for living, the insane character of that daily agitation, and uselessness of suffering' (1964, 6). Then, in a universe 'suddenly divested of illusions and lights, man feels an alien, a stranger' (1964). Meaning cannot be found either outside or within the world. In Camus's analysis of Kierkegaard's response to the absurd, he sees that his leap tries to escape from that judgement; it 'makes of the absurd the criterion of the other world, whereas it is simply a residue of the experience of this world' (38). Whilst there may be a desire for God, a nostalgia for unity, this can never be and just compounds the absurdity.

Yet Camus is not able to escape religious explanations even as he either rejects them or later brings them within the world. It is pertinent that in both texts, it is in reaction to religious accounts of existence that his absurd heroes make their stand. The absurd, he quips, is 'sin without God' (40), and even in trying to escape this, with existential philosophers having their God in negation and mystics losing themselves in their God and gaining some peace in that slavery, it remains. The absurd man must not follow the path of the mystic. He draws instead three consequences from the absurd: my revolt, my freedom, and my passion. The absurd man goes beyond God and the mystics, noting that response but living outside it.

Camus ends the essay with a reflection on the eternal, futile task of Sisyphus who, for his rebellion against the gods, was condemned to roll a rock up a hill for all eternity only for it to immediately roll down again. Sisyphus is the absurd hero, who does not despair of his situation nor run from it but continues in defiance of it, teaching 'the higher fidelity that negates the gods and raises rocks. He too concludes that all is well' (123). The struggle that he has toward the heights is 'enough to fill a man's heart'; one must imagine Sisyphus happy (123).

The engagement therewith the figure of God is more sympathetic than Meursault's assault of the chaplain. Camus's sympathy for this vision informs his own rejection of Sartrean existentialism. Commenting on *Being and Nothingness*, he argues that Christianity is preferable to it. Existentialism 'does not suppose a mode of conduct' (Camus 1966, 38), whereas Christianity espouses 'the duty to love' (Camus 1963, 54). This concern with and knowledge of Christianity is a surprisingly constant strand in Camus's writing, with the themes and analysis of his MA thesis on the Christian reception of Greek thought reappearing in his second philosophical essay *The Rebel*. This is not to smuggle Camus into Christianity, as Aronson sees others as doing (Aronson 2012). Whilst I am wary of taking an MA thesis as definitive for someone's thought, the persistence of themes and the analysis from it in later work adds weight to doing so.

In his introduction to the text, Srigley notes that the subject of Camus's final, uncompleted cycle Nemesis would engage with the subject and themes of the thesis. The text can therefore illustrate 'both Camus' uneasiness about Christianity and his inability to escape its assumptions completely' (Srigley 2007, 28). These include the prioritisation of immanentism over transcendence, the importance of the questions of evil and death in Augustine, and the abandonment of man to the grace of Christ (Camus 2007, 128). Other concerns are over the active rather than passive nature of faith, that kind of 'inner asceticism that amounts to accepting faith' (Camus 2007, 132).[26] These central concerns are reflected in both *The Myth of Sisyphus* and *The Rebel*.

---

[26] Kirkpatrick and Pattison see that this work sets the scene for his later engagement with questions such as 'the problem of evil; whether we say yes or not the world in Nietzschean affirmation or Christian negation; whether we belong it; the desire for God and the need for coherence; the role of reason, whether "rational" or "mystic"; whether the only freedom available to us is the freedom to sin' (Kirkpatrick and Pattison 2018, 141). Camus ends his text with the curious

The Rebel begins with a reflection on the absurd, which takes on the role of the Cartesian cogito. It 'wipes the slate clean' (Camus 1951, 22); it is the starting point of consciousness. This twist on the cogito continues, and revolt is the first piece of evidence that 'pulls the individual from their solitude. It is a communal place that is founded on humanity as the first value. I rebel, therefore I am' (36). Rebellion and revolt are seen as universal and constant aspects of human life, and our relationship to them is examined historically, philosophically, and politically.

Thus, we see a central instance of Camus's separation from the existentialists: the affirmation of a communal human project and of human nature. Hence, Camus stands outside of Webber's definition as he 'believes in an emotional fraternity inherent in human nature' (Webber 2018, 34). Human nature is constituted by this emotional concern for others and the duty to love. *The Rebel* moderates the individualism of Sisyphus and *L'Étranger*: from those experiences of the absurd suffering is individual, 'but from the movement of rebellion, it becomes collective, it is an adventure of all' (Camus 1951, 36). For if the revolt is awareness of limit, a boundary that is known even by a slave, a cry against injustice, then there is a communal sense of value. From this sense of value can come duties, such as the duty to love. In revolt, throughout the ages, 'we find a value judgement in the name of which the rebel refuses to approve the condition in which he is found' (39).

In *The Rebel*, there are certain ambiguities over Christianity and its response to modernity, particularly in the analysis of the rebel's relationship to the divine. The rebel is both set up in contrast to God and in line with God, where 'only two possible universes exist for the human spirit, the sacred (or to speak in Christian terms, of grace) and that of rebellion' (34). In the section on metaphysical rebellion, it appears necessary for the rebel to revolt against God, that man should protest metaphysically 'against his condition and the entirety of creation'. One should contest 'the ends of humanity and of creation' (39) and revolt against 'the suffering of life and death'. Whilst the metaphysical rebel may not necessarily be an atheist, they are necessarily a blasphemer 'primarily in the name of order, denouncing God as the father of death and the supreme scandal' (40).

Yet, once this metaphysical rebellion has taken place and God has been vanquished, this fall must be justified, often so violently and oppressively. Once morality and values are destroyed in this manner, 'God is no longer the guarantee of our existence, man must himself determine the fact, in order to be'

comment that Christianity 'remains the only common hope and only effective shield against the calamity of the Western world. Christian thought had conquered through its universality' (2008, 133).

(84). Camus sees that the figure of God, this personal, responsible creator, is inextricable from the urge to rebel and that 'we can say thus, without being paradoxical, that the history of rebellion in the Western world is inseparable from that of Christianity' (46).

Christianity itself contains a metaphysical rebellion in the death of Christ on the cross, although it is rendered useless through the resurrection, the Kingdom of God, and eternal life. Christ also came, Camus notes, to solve evil and death, the problems that the rebel engages with. Man cries for justice when confronted with evil and death, but Christianity cannot respond as it moves towards eternal life and demands faith. Yet the rebel, like the believer, is the one who dreams of unity and totality and projects that ideal horizontally onto a world deprived of God.

This perhaps makes more sense of Camus's avowal that 'I do not believe in God and I am not an atheist' (Camus 2008, 112), and his comment that to resolve the problems of modernity, one must 'go back to the passage from Hellenism to Christianity, the true and only turning point in history' (1966, 267). This ambiguity about and wrestling with aspects of God continues in his last published novel *The Fall*, an excoriating account of human nature, its evasions, its desires, and attempts at solutions.[27] Formed of a series of monologues, we are party to one side of a conversation in which the protagonist, Jean-Baptiste Clamence, details his life to a stranger in an Amsterdam bar. Once a successful lawyer in Paris, he now styles himself as a *juge-pénitent*. Having been haunted by the sound of laughter, he develops a certain self-consciousness that he tries to exorcise. The novel is saturated with theological themes, from its title to the allusions to the seven circles of hell to the presence of a stolen panel of the Ghent altarpiece. In the climax of the book, Clamence speaks of our drive to be ruled, to be absolved, but as 'God is no longer in fashion' (Camus 1956, 154), we are all sin, no grace. And yet we want grace (156).

He confesses that he is attempting to atone for his inaction in preventing a young woman from jumping to her death from a bridge. To do so, he sets himself up as an ersatz God, where through his constant confession and accusation of himself, and the narration of it to others, he can judge others, as they themselves confess in response to Clamence's confession. Yet Clamence cannot grant any forgiveness, and his narration drives home the lack of innocence and universal guilt of all humanity. Although throughout the novel there is a cry for solidarity and for humanism, it ends with Clamence's admission that even given

---

[27] What *The Fall* wants to communicate is the subject of debate: Sprintzen (2020, 248) sees it as a 'dramatic depiction' and critique of the bourgeois individualism of *Being and Nothingness*, whereas Whistler extracts a more positive vision of human solidarity from it (2018, 60).

again the chance to save the woman, he may not take it. After all, the water is so cold.

Camus wrote in his diaries that 'if, to outgrow nihilism, one must return to Christianity, one may well follow the impulse and outgrow Christianity in Hellenism' (Camus 1966, 183). In outgrowing his nihilism, Camus engages with Christianity, although whether he returns to Hellenism is contestable.[28] Camus's engagement with monotheism takes a different form to Sartre and Beauvoir's: Sartre sees that Camus's understanding of the absurd arises from a desire for God,[29] a desire that McBride sees is a constant in Camus's thought (McBride 1992, 175–177).

Other analyses of Camus's relationship to religion see that it results in an immanent mystical affirmation and openness that correlate with the ontological promises of monotheism.[30] There are glimpses of this at the end of *L'Étranger*, where although Meursault does not see Christ in the stones of the prison, he is stirred by the sky, stars, and the benign indifference of the world, achieving a kind of peace. Camus himself writes of a mystical experience in the essay 'Summer in Algiers', albeit an immanent one where

> Unity expresses itself here in terms of sea and sky. The heart senses it through a certain taste of the flesh that constitutes its bitterness and greatness. I am learning that there is no superhuman happiness, no eternity outside the curve of the days . . . Not that we should behave as beasts, but I can see no point in the happiness of angels. All I know is that this sky will last longer than I shall. And what can I call eternity except what will continue after my death? . . . to

---

[28] Per Archambault: 'if it be a Christian disease to feel dispossessed and cast adrift in a hostile universe, it is fair to say that, although Camus fought that disease tooth and nail, he never entirely convalesced . . . I am rather inclined to think, however, that his metaphysical malaise was more Gnostic than Christian, the product, as it were, of a Graeco-Christian germ' (1972, 104).

[29] 'But since, according to your own terms, injustice is eternal—that is to say, since the absence of God is a constant through the changes of history—the immediate relation, which is always begun anew, of the man who demands to have a meaning (that is to say, that a meaning be given to him), to this God, who remains eternally silent, itself transcends History. The tension through which man realizes himself—which is, at the same time, an intuitive joy of being—is therefore a veritable conversion that he snatches from everyday "restlessness" and from "history" in order to make it coincide finally with his condition. One can go no farther; no progress can find a place in this instantaneous tragedy' (Sartre 1952, 346). See also Cruickshank's comment that 'what makes Camus so significant, and in many ways representative, a figure of his own generation is the fact that he experienced a religious need in its widest sense yet was unable to accept religious belief' (Cruickshank 1967, 324).

[30] See Whistler 2018, who writes 'this horizontal transcendence is therefore somewhat pantheistic, as all the spiritual feeling and profundity of emotion that humanity experiences is part of our physical world'(57), and Kirkpatrick and Pattison who note that even with the Nietzschean ending of Camus's MA thesis, 'against Nietzsche's claim that Christianity's ascetic ideal involved "saying no to life", Camus's exploration of the relation between Christianity, Hellenism, and modernity led him to conclude that there was a mystical way of saying yes to life' (Kirkpatrick and Pattison 2018, 135).

be pure means to rediscover that country of the soul where one's kinship with
the world can be felt, where the throbbing of one's blood mingles with the
violent pulsations of the afternoon sun. (Camus 1970, 90)

Yet, whilst Camus may find these moments of mystical peace and transcendence, I argue that a more consistent vision is offered by The Fall. This text
presents perhaps a more honest account of human nature: its desires and its
failures, and may be aware that the defiance and rebellion of his earlier works
lead to fragmentation and alienation. For if we are only on earth, we are ever
situated in our relational, responsible quandaries and their failures. Even if we
seek rest and solace in the sun, the sea, or the stars, the laughter follows us, and
in the laughter, the fall.

3.4 Conclusion

I have explored two thinkers who count as existentialists proper and another
who shares some of their concerns whilst rejecting a central aspect of their
analysis of human existence and nature. I now return to the central, ontological
slogan of existentialism: that existence precedes essence. For existentialism to
be existentialism proper, it must be ontologically dependent on that statement:
indeed, the philosophies of Sartre and Beauvoir are. I have shown how they
argue that this statement is inherently atheistic. In the following section, I will
argue that it is in fact compatible with theism.

I conclude this discussion by further detailing the relationship of this atheistic
existentialism to monotheism. Two recent works have sought to define existentialism in terms of praxis (Khawaja 2016; Webber 2018). In redefining existentialism as a tradition rather than a movement, Khawaja argues that it should be
seen as 'a pattern of intergenerational influence, in which later figures read and
appropriated the work of earlier figures' (2016, 4). As a tradition, it resem-
blances a religion: not only through shared concepts and ideals but also in its
character. Existentialism is the struggle and ascetic practice of authenticity, and
this idea of personal authenticity is 'at the center of existential thought' (2016,
24).

In Crowell's recent account of existentialism, he sees that Khawaja's encompassing approach mirrors Webber's more ethically specific one in its outworking: with the affirmation of authenticity as an ethic and personal mandate. Thus,
we helpfully have three recent accounts that emphasise different aspects of
existentialism in both practical and genealogical ways: as ethical and psychological (Webber 2018), as concerned with phenomenology and its method
(Crowell 2020), and as a ritual or practical outworking (Khawaja 2016).
Through the discussion about the relationship that existentialism proper has

with monotheism, I argue there can be another way to conceive of existentialism and differentiate it. This involves moving from the practice and method of existentialism to look at not just its genealogical reliance on monotheism but the way in which the ontological vision of existentialism came to be.

If we define existentialism as ontologically dependent on the statement that existence precedes essence, then the ontological status of God is caught up in it. This approach is one that is attentive to the foundational texts of existentialism proper and to the serious ontological claims being made. I see this as a return to the source of existentialism, which is to explore the nature of human existence, even if it means rejecting an account of it having a nature or an essence. To further explore the relationship of God to these questions of essence and existence, I turn now to how religious thinkers enveloped under existentialism navigated this question, both before and in light of the works just discussed.

4 God beyond Being and Nothingness

Having centred the definition of existentialism proper as thought that engages and explores, ontologically, what it means for existence to precede essence, I am able to more fully relate certain religious thinkers to existentialism in a way that will not shortchange or elide their thought. Although Sartre admits that Christian existentialists hold to the idea that existence precedes essence, he makes it clear in 'Existentialism is a Humanism' that he regards them as living in bad faith. After all, he reasons, if there is a God, then essence must precede existence. This judgement, and the popularity of atheistic existentialism as characterised by Sartre and Beauvoir, alongside the work of Camus, has had an impact on how theistic existentialism has been interpreted and been judged to be improper existentialism.[31] If Christianity, or God is brought in, then human freedom is compromised; human essence is set; and our radical or responsible freedom is an impossibility.

As this following exploration of religious, and specifically Christian, existentialism will show, that judgement is faulty. The Christian existentialists I explore here both precede and succeed the moment of atheistic existentialism, and their engagement with that form of existentialism reveals that the charges levelled at theism by the atheistic existentialists often caricature the nature and role of God in theistic accounts of existence. Not only is the basic character of existentialism proper anticipated and explored by Christian existentialism, but their thought also engages with and provides responses to the often

---

[31] Cruickshank comments that 'one inclines more and more to the view that the movement does not possess the means of becoming a Christian philosophy without changing its basic character' (Cruickshank 1957, 64). Grene sees that whilst Marcel and Jaspers's vision of existence is 'apparently more gentler and cheerful', it is also 'infinitely duller' (Grene 1948, 140).

underdeveloped accounts of God rejected in existentialism proper. I underscore, however, that the systems of Christian existentialists are not reducible to a response to atheistic existentialism. Instead, they often present a different vision entirely from their own accounts of the experience of isolated and abandoned humanity.[32]

I have chosen the following thinkers, Gabriel Marcel, Nikolai Berdyaev, and Paul Tillich, for two reasons. The first is that they all espouse an ontology in which existence precedes essence and can thus be counted as existentialists proper: bad faith or not. The second is that their engagement with existentialism began prior to and continued past the existentialism that was successfully propagated by Sartre, Beauvoir, and others in the so-called existentialist café. The sources of their existentialism proper in some instances came about independently of the usual existentialist genealogy, preceding the reception of Kierkegaard, Heidegger, and Jaspers in France, sourced instead in the French Augustinian tradition or through Jakob Boehme and Schelling.

These thinkers also all engaged fulsomely with proto-existentialists such as Kierkegaard, Heidegger, and Jaspers. They thus engage with the questions they raise concerning essence and existence. Their thought should therefore be counted as existentialism proper, standing as both independent of and responsive to the existentialism of Sartre and Beauvoir. Their disagreements with atheistic existentialism are evidence of the engagement and compatibility of existentialism with monotheism, and through standing inside rather than outside, they can respond to the claim that, echoing and altering Heidegger, Christian existentialism is a round square or a misunderstanding.

Secondly, whilst they all subscribe to a Christian vision of existence, they represent different traditions of Christianity, being Roman Catholic, Russian Orthodox, and German Lutheran in turn. This is not to say that they are archetypal representatives of these traditions, as each thinker stood somewhat uneasily within their respective traditions. Indeed, it may be said that there is a scope to Christian existentialism such that its existence precedes comments on its essence. It is certainly evidence that existentialism proper cannot be seen as incompatible with monotheism. Instead, the presence of God in existentialism can contextualise the vision of life presented by the existentialism proper explored above whilst not abandoning the central ontological claim that existence precedes essence.

---

[32] Pax notes that the unifying factor is not God but instead 'the perception of man as experientially incomplete in himself' (Pax 1972, 93).

4.1 Gabriel Marcel (1888–1973): Being and Mystery

I turn first to Gabriel Marcel, who played a central role in the intellectual and cultural scene of Paris. Alongside hosting a weekly philosophical salon at which a number of our existentialists and their contemporaries were present (such as Jean Wahl, Nikolai Berdyaev, Simone de Beauvoir, Jean-Paul Sartre, Emmanuel Levinas, and Paul Ricoeur), he wrote plays as well as more overtly philosophical works. In his philosophical works, Marcel often expounds upon themes explored in his plays, and in an autobiographical essay laments that it was his philosophical, rather than theatrical, work that made him famous. He did not have a religious upbringing, and his 1929 conversion to Catholicism was brought about by the author François Mauriac. Having observed a number of particularly Catholic themes and concerns in Marcel's work, he wrote to Marcel asking him whether he ought not to join the Catholic Church.

Marcel's relationship with the cultural moment of existentialism is somewhat ambivalent. Although he initially endorsed it and is reputed to have coined it, he later strongly disavowed it, writing that 'I do not believe I have ever made use of the term existentialism in my writings; besides, I suspect that the idea of existentialism implies a contradiction, for I do not see how a philosophy of existence worthy of the name could be an "ism"' (Marcel 1984, 49). Despite this disavowal, he may well have been the first to use it in France around 1943, having set out its lines in the 1925 essay 'Existence and Objectivity'. Yet, when Marcel was labelled a Christian existentialist by Sartre 1945, he was surprised by this and reluctant to be associated with Sartre's existentialism, for 'the term *existentialism* engendered the most unfortunate associations of ideas in the mind of the average reader' (Marcel 1984, 48). Moreover, his exploration of existentialist themes and ideas occurred independently of the reception of Kierkegaard and Heidegger in France, instead being a reaction against aspects of German Idealism that discounted existence in favour of abstract being, and Neo-Thomism's neglect of the person in their present time. He later incorporated aspects of Kierkegaard and Heidegger's accounts of existence, transcendence, and being into his thought.

Marcel's philosophy is not particularly systematic, to which the diaristic nature of his *Journal métaphysique* and the first part of *Being and Having* attest. Despite its unsystematic nature, the strains of his thought are fairly constant. Marcel writes that 'the essence of man is to be in a situation' (1964, 83), and he observes that 'from the beginning my researches were explicitly directed towards what might be called the concrete examination of the individual and of the transcendent, as opposed to all idealism based on the impersonal or the immanent' (1962, 137). Marcel explores the uneasy, restless situation of the individual and their relationships: with themselves, others, and the world, taking a phenomenological approach that always incorporates the body in the act of thinking (hence his preference for the German phrase *es denkt in mir* to the *cogito ergo sum*).

We find that we are situated, involved in Being. We simply *are*, and from that, we need to relate ourselves: to ourselves, to others, to 'plenary Reality' (1949, 35). Marcel's philosophical method rejects the distinction between essence and existence. The distinction is merely a way of presenting the relationship between thought and reality, and as thought can never get outside of existence the transition is illusory. Instead, thought is a self-transcendence as we are always already in relation to being. From this situated, embodied starting point, we have two particular postures to take in relation to the situation in which we find ourselves. These are *disponibilité* and *indisponibilité*:[33] to be either open and available or closed off and self-conscious. If we are *disponible*, we are able to see the other person as a Thou, rather than as something to be used for our own ends. If we are *indisponible*, or in the presence of someone *indisponible*, it is as if we are 'with someone for whom I do not exist, and so I am thrown back on myself' (1949, 72). This corresponds to whether we engage in being or having: whether we resist dissolution or take up a grasping approach to the world.

As humans in a broken world, we seek to justify ourselves and our existence, to produce ourselves and establish ourselves by our acts. We want confirmation and recognition from those outside ourselves. Both our freedom and our desire to know our worth are, for Marcel, what our relationship with God hinges on. We have an urgent need and drive for being and for transcending as we are not at home with ourselves. The tragedy of life lies 'in our desperate efforts to make ourselves as one with something which nevertheless is not, and cannot, be identical with our beings' (1951, 98). This desire to know our worth is an appeal, sent out in a movement of transcendence 'towards one who can only be described as an absolute Thou, a last and supreme resource for the troubled human spirit' (1951, 152). Our freedom is not the freedom to act, but rather the freedom to be a certain way. It is linked to our relationality rather than in conflict with it.

The freedom we have is either to assert being or to deny it. This is Marcel's navigation of relationality, which starts on a more optimistic grounding than Sartre's. To be a person, to make that free choice, we take on responsibility: to ourselves and to everyone else. We establish ourselves as a person only 'in so far

---

[33] You will find this term translated variously as disposibility, handiness (Marcel's preferred), availability, or receptivity. I am leaving it untranslated in order to bring out its meaning through its use in the language.

as I really believe in the existence of others and allow this belief to influence my conduct' (1962, 22). As we already 'in being', we do not base ourselves on ourselves and then go out to the other from there. If we are to ground ourselves on something such that we can relate to others well, we must ground ourselves on the mystery of hope. If we deny this and try and base ourselves on ourselves, we become solipsistic: self-conscious and self-centred. In denying hope, we take up an attitude of pessimistic fatalism.

As a mystery, hope is undefinable and indescribable. Yet the possibility of hope is also the necessity of despair, and we can explore what hope is through negating what despair is. Despair is to renounce the idea of remaining oneself, to be fascinated by 'the idea of one's own destruction to the point of anticipating this very destruction itself' (1962, 38). In contrast, the person who hopes is *disponible*: they can set no condition and abandon themselves in absolute confidence. They would 'thus transcend all possible disappointment and would experience a security of his being, or in his being, which is contrary to the radical insecurity of Having'. Hope is an ontological position, one which is inseparable from a faith which is 'likewise absolute, transcending all laying down of conditions' (1962, 46).

Hope is also related to God, as the source of this hope is the response of the creature to the absolute Thou. The absolute Thou brings us out of nothingness such that 'I implicitly accept the possibility of despair as an indication of treason, so that I could not give way to it without pronouncing my own condemnation' (1962, 47). To move into this despair is to ally oneself with having, to shut ourselves off from hope and abandon ourselves to anxiety. It is a move into oneself, as hope is linked to communion, grounding our relationships with others.

This faith and hope further impact our relationship with ourselves, for our own presence to ourselves must 'constantly be reconquered' through our fidelity to ourselves. That creative fidelity to life, to hope, and openness to those around us bespeaks of a different relationship to death than found, he notes, in Heidegger and Jaspers. Instead of directing our being towards death or realising it in relation to death, we actively negate it with fidelity and, through that fidelity, exercise a love that rejects closed systems, passes beyond itself, and 'demands for its complete realisation a universal communion outside which it cannot be satisfied and is destined to be corrupted and lost in the end' (1962, 152). This project can only be centred upon the absolute Thou of God.

Thus, Marcel's account of freedom is one that plays with passivity and activity: we choose to be *disponible*, to be open and receptive. Although within the world I may be 'condemned to make my calculations with cooked figures', the response is not merely to square up to that fact, but instead to discover the conditions 'under which the real balance-sheet may occasionally emerge in a partial and temporary fashion from underneath the cooked figures that mask it' (1951, 168). Marcel starts in our situatedness, where we pre-exist ourselves, and sees that from there we should move towards the *disponibilité* of intersubjectivity rather than retreat into the self-consciousness of *indisponibilité*.

Marcel's understanding of existence and being appears in many ways the antithesis of the Sartrean account, with its focus on relationality as possible and transcendence as having an end. It is also an account that can bear on Beauvoir's situatedness and sedimentation. Marcel's 1943 review of *Being and Nothingness* tracks along these lines. Although acknowledging it as an important work, he sees that Sartre rejects the authentic transcending 'by which we break free from these facts and these conditions and substitute for them renewed facts and conditions'. This is the merit of Sartre's work: it shows us clearly, without any doubts, 'a form of metaphysics which denies or refuses grace', one that sets in front of us an 'image of an atrophied and contradictory world where the better part of ourselves is finally unable to recognise itself' (1962, 183). It is a picture of the world that constantly rejects love, projects refusal and individuality, and is utterly intoxicated with itself.

Marcel extends similar criticisms to Camus's absurd, seeing it as a vision that 'refuses to imagine a metaphysical background from which some light might shine forth to transfigure the scene. It refuses, out of honesty in the first place, but also out of pride, and we have there two states of mind so closely interconnected that we cannot think of separating them' (1962, 205). What appears as defiance is, in fact, individualism and pride. We are left with a 'Narcissism of nothingness', with nothing other than to 'wonder tirelessly at our courage, our pride and our stubbornness in denying both God and the being full of weakness and hope which in spite of everything and for ever we are' (1962, 213).

Marcel explores the world of the atheistic existentialists and finds it true up to a point: it is a world of having rather than being. Therefore, the metaphysical and ontological vision put forward is not the absolutely honest look that they claim it is but is instead a refusal to countenance and explore an openness, a rejection of love, hope, and relationality. The individual and their rebellion may be a starting point, but the call, for Marcel, is to turn outwards rather than inwards, from isolation and self-consciousness towards the mysteries of being, love, and hope. The move towards *disponibilité* rather than *indisponibilité* is possible because being is always a mystery: ungraspable, undefinable, and therefore not set.

Hence, Marcel's desire to disentangle himself from existentialism à la Sartre. Marcel's analysis of existence and his response to it sheds light on how complicated the conversation around monotheism and existentialism can be.

Throughout 'Existentialism is a Humanism', Christian existentialism is seen as that which sets limits and boundaries for human existence. It gives it an essence and promotes passivity in the individual and towards the world. Yet Marcel always sought to reject strict, set essences, instead calling for the openness and availability of the subject to the mystery of being. What Sartre rejects is not the full story of God's possible relation to the world for Marcel. Instead, he sees that Sartre ends up with an autonomous, having human subject that is unable to see outside itself. The use of autonomy is key: Marcel distinguishes between autonomy and freedom, with the latter linked to *disponibilité*. The more I freely enter into the whole of an activity with the whole of myself, the less legitimate it is to say that I am autonomous (1949, 173).

This is not to say that Marcel's philosophy 'solves' the problems of Sartre, nor would Marcel want to be seen as doing so. Yet this discussion has shown not only that Marcel's work and vision can be incorporated into existentialism proper, but it has illustrated how existentialism proper is compatible with monotheism. Marcel's thought is existentialist in its focus on the individual in their situation; in its exploration of the anxiety that the human being faces in relation to their possibilities in the world; in rejecting the idea of a set human essence; and in underscoring the importance of freedom and responsibility. Yet the idea of God in Marcel opens up the possibility not only of acknowledging the brokenness of the world but also of transcending it, even in an impossible, ungraspable way.

4.2 Nikolai Berdyaev (1874–1943): Creativity ex nihilo

I turn now to another contemporary of Marcel and Sartre, the Russian philosopher Nikolai Berdyaev. Having been exiled on the famous philosophers' ships from Russia in the 1920s, he settled eventually in Paris. Berdyaev's philosophy, sourced from both Russian and Western thought, engages with existentialist questions and concerns such as the importance of freedom, the restless, bifurcated nature of humanity, and the spur of anxiety. Although he will define existentialism as coming out of Kierkegaard's focus on the individual and truth as subjectivity (1947), he relates that he saw himself as an existentialist 'before I even came to know of Kierkegaard's writings' (1950, 102). His thought is instead shaped by Jakob Boehme and Schelling, as well as engaging both positively and negatively with the work of thinkers such as Pascal, Nietzsche, Dostoevsky, Tolstoy, Kierkegaard, and Heidegger.

Berdyaev's thought uses aspects of existential philosophy such as Kierkegaard's truth as subjectivity, the effect of anxiety, the disjointed experience of consciousness, and the importance of freedom. Thus, a number of his philosophical and religious concerns correspond with the existentialism found in Left Bank cafés and bars. However, he saw that as merely fashionable and that popularity as the death of any serious philosophy. Whilst he responds to and engages with that variant of existentialism in his later work, his response reiterates much of what he had formulated in earlier works. Berdyaev rejects the phenomenological method that lies behind certain existentialists as fundamentally objectifying, shutting its eyes 'to the mystery of the life of man, of the world, and of God' (1949, v). He initially dismisses the thought of Sartre and Camus as drawing on, in the face of nothingness, the spirit of neo-humanism. For Berdyaev, we must resolve our nausea by turning towards the supernatural in the natural.

Berdyaev's definition of existentialist philosophy is that it is a philosophical position that does not objectify knowledge, where objectification means 'alienation, loss of individuality, loss of freedom, subjection to the common, and cognition by means of the concept' (1953, 11). Existentialist philosophy is also expressionist; it expresses 'the existentiality of the cognitive mind rather than something abstracted from that existentiality' (1953, 12). There is further an emphasis on freedom, where *Existenz* 'in its depth is freedom' (1953, 12). Berdyaev sees that these emphases disappear in the existentialisms of Sartre or Heidegger. The personalist, integral vision of humanity disappears in Heidegger's philosophy of nothing as it seeks to discover the structure of being in human existence. Heidegger and Sartre are 'in the grip of objectifying knowledge', failing to 'break with the tradition which comes down from Parmenides' (1953, 12).[34] They remain resolutely in the world of things as they deny the 'primary reality of spiritual experience' (1953, 15), explaining humanity from below. Their understanding of human existence is only half the story, as they are blind to grace, the 'divine element in man, the eternal bond between transcendental man and God' (1953, 23). For Berdyaev that is an incomplete picture of the world, and if they remain there, in their bleak vision, they are closed off from truth. In contrast, Berdyaev talks of the transcendental human, who exists beyond the duality of subject and object, open to the divine with the 'a priori of religion' (1953, 17).

Berdyaev sees that human existence is composed of two irreconcilable realities. In *The Meaning of the Creative Act*, Berdyaev contrasts the 'given world of necessity' (1962, 11) with the divine in human nature that stands over and against that world. We are both in and not of the world; we exist in an 'eternal antinomy of transcendent and immanent, of dualism and monism'

---

[34] This is a bit unfair on Heidegger, as Berdyaev does acknowledge later. Berdyaev's reading of Kierkegaard tends to focus on his account of anxiety and perhaps conflates it too much with fear (cf. Pattison 2020).

(1962, 15). We are conscious of the splits in our nature. We know that we are powerful but weak, of worth but worthless, natural but eternal, that '*in his essence, man is a break in the world of nature, he cannot be contained within it*' (1962, 60). Within us, there is a lack of unity, a non-being that is the source of our disjunction with the world. Yet it is also the source of our creative action and our freedom.

Berdyaev's transcendental human is the free human: free from static concepts of being, God, nature, society, history, and civilization, amongst others. Freedom, in Berdyaev, stems from Boehme's heterodox concept of the *Ungrund*, a concept Schelling's later philosophy draws on. In Boehme's vision, God does not create the world ex nihilo but wills himself into existence from the void of nothingness that is the *Ungrund*. From this act of will, God will later transform and modulate into the Trinity. This account of God prevents God from being associated with being because one cannot say that God *is*. Instead, as Berdyaev comments, the vision is '*nothingness* as distinct from *something* in order of being'. It is a 'primal pre-existential freedom' that precedes being and is beyond the world of causality (1939, 144–145). This freedom is meontic, sourced in and from nothing.

Freedom, far from being hemmed in on by God, is guaranteed by God and finds its source in God. It springs from our non-being, which is the source of creativity. Created as we are in God's image and likeness, we have this will to create, called as we are to free, spontaneous activity and not a passive submission to God. This creativeness, as the exercise of our freedom, is our own creating out of nothingness, although unlike God we cannot create life or matter from nothing. This places us as both the riddle of and the solution to the universe. Full as we are of unresolvable paradoxes and living in a fallen world, we are to exercise our creativity and create our ethical existence, orientated towards the future even as we are involved in history and its failures. We are not called on to follow particular moral laws but to exercise our freedom and 'co-operate with God, to create the good and produce new values' (1960, 44). As the break in the natural world, we can work with that and relate to the supernatural reality to which it points.

Thus, the self-contradictory, fraught nature of humanity is not our useless passion but a spur to our creativity. Berdyaev notes that we long for both salvation and creativity, we desire to be passive but need to be active, and we are to work out our own salvation in fear and trembling. We are the image and likeness of God, containing a 'Divine idea which his freedom may realize or destroy' (1960, 53). Berdyaev's ethics are also personalistic, which again he saw as essential to existential philosophy (1947, 51). Personality, for Berdyaev, is something that is tied up in the spiritual world; it is 'the highest hierarchical value in the world, a value of the spiritual order' (1960, 55). The personality is 'eternal, identical and unique' as well as 'permanently in a process of creative change'; its content is 'best revealed in love' (1947, 122, 128, 146). This love presupposes another personality to which our personality must relate and enables an I-Thou relationship that aspires towards communion. That community, the *sobernost*, is founded on an ethics that begins 'by opposing the final socialization of man which destroys the freedom of spirit and conscience' (1960, 58).

This love is sourced from God. It is a force, a 'radiation of beneficent, life-giving energy' that is 'divinely human and is the interaction between man and God' (1960, 117). Our individual creativity opens the infinite up into the finite and points towards what the idea of God for humanity is: to be infinite, free, creative, and loving, focused on the concrete and individual. Love, as the content of freedom, leads us to an individuality of the new Adam, not the old freedom of individualism. It calls us to imitate Christ, himself a union of the divine and the human who instantiated a new anthropology that humanity can participate in, the Absolute Man who redeems and saves human nature.

By denying this primordial spirituality, the truth proposed by the atheistic existentialists can only ever be objectifying. It is only the transcendental vision of the human, as beyond the duality of subject and object, that can experience the truth. Truth is existential; it is not an object out there in the world or a framework. Instead, 'in its ultimate depth Truth is God and God is Truth' (1953, 26); it is a creative discovery, and this is why atheistic existentialism is objectifying. The subjectivity of Heidegger and Sartre remains in the objectified world and is therefore a philosophy of profound pessimism, of *néant*. Sartre's philosophy comes in for particular virulent criticism from Berdyaev, being 'flat and vile' (1949, 95), with his novels describing only 'filth and degradation' (1953, 110).

Berdyaev notes that Sartre later declares himself an optimist, making an 'appeal to man's sense of responsibility and to his activity and endows him with freedom through which he can fashion a better life' (1953, 110). Yet Berdyaev reasons that Sartre's ontology makes this an impossibility as Sartre's freedom from nothing is ontologically faulty. Berdyaev is able to instantiate a creative, positive freedom from nothing as freedom is sourced in the primordial *Ungrund*. However, in Sartre, as God is the enemy of humans, his freedom has to be naturalistic. Sartre describes nothingness as the worm in the apple which rots it; the freedom of nothingness comes after being, corrupting it. Therefore, it is 'incapable of giving birth to anything positive', it is a freedom that 'leads to no result and has no aim in view'. The fundamental mistake of

Sartre is his 'unwillingness to admit that denial presupposes an assertion of something positive' (1953, 111).

Berdyaev's philosophical vision provides a direct, ontological challenge to the vision of Sartre. Whilst his reading of Kierkegaard and Heidegger is at times too dismissive and his analysis of Sartre vituperative, there is an ontological issue that Berdyaev has identified. The ontology of Sartre's freedom, both before and after his agreement with Beauvoir, is flawed. If both Sartre and Beauvoir want to have freedom as a positive value, as the goal for humanity, and if we are to be responsible for the freedom of others, then their actual, ontological position, where freedom is nothingness, cannot sustain it. Beauvoir's ethics take Sartre's ontology as their starting point, and whilst Sartre's ethics view of freedom changes he never adjusts his ontology to fit with it. In contrast to them, in Berdyaev it is God who is the guarantee of freedom, where 'if there is no God then I am the slave of the world. The existence of God is the guarantee of my independence of the world, of society, of the State' (1949, 136). The meontic freedom of God is primordial, not parasitic, whereas without God we remain in the world of necessity, trapped in objectivity and objectifying.

4.3 Paul Tillich (1886–1965): The Ground and Power of Being

Of the three Christian existentialists we have explored, Paul Tillich is the one who is most explicitly and intimately involved in theology, although he rejected the label of the existentialist theologian. Tillich sought to bring theology and culture into constant dialogue with one another with his method of correlation, where the concerns of the day are to be correlated with the symbols used in the Christian message. The theologian is to engage with the questions and concerns of existence as they come up in philosophy, in art, and in culture. Through engaging these questions and concerns, theology can transform existence in response to the anxieties of the age, manifested in the culture of the age.

After his experiences as a chaplain in World War I, Tillich began his teaching career in Berlin, often relating philosophy of religion and theology to contemporary themes in culture, such as philosophy, politics, art, psychology, and sociology. When appointed to Marburg in 1924, he came into contact with Heidegger and his burgeoning philosophy. Tillich saw it as a particular pattern of thought that could be traced back to Hegel, Schelling, and Kierkegaard, and Tillich's own existentialism is as much due to his work on Schelling as his encounters with Heidegger.[35] As it was part of the culture and the philosophy of the time, Tillich's theology engages with and responds to key existentialist

---

[35] See Pattison 2015, 27n8.

claims: that existence precedes essence; that nothingness pervades our being; that human existence is estranged and anxious; and the importance of freedom.

Tillich sees that if one is to engage with and correlate theology to the existentialist vision, an ontology based on set and static essences must be jettisoned. That vision cannot speak to the philosophical concerns of the day, and so one cannot return to Augustine's vision of existence and the rest that is espoused there (2014, 128). Composed as we are of being and non-being, Tillich sees that the question of our being arises out of the 'the shock of possible non-being' (2012, 181). This is when the individual realises that they are thrown towards death and the cessation of their being. This threat of non-being sparks anxiety, where we realise that we are not 'able to preserve one's own being' (2014, 37). This basic anxiety cannot be eliminated: it 'belongs to existence itself' (2014, 38). The anxiety of non-being manifests ontically, spiritually, and morally, corresponding to anxieties about death, meaninglessness, guilt and condemnation, which characterise existence.

Whilst our existence stands 'out of non-being' (2013, 23), the state of existence is 'the state of estrangement' (2013, 51); being has priority, ontologically, over non-being. Non-being is therefore dependent on being. This separation, for Tillich, is not just the bare fact of life that can never be resolved but speaks to a unity that the existential self wishes to regain, the quest for 'essentialization'. This quest is the desire for God, but not a God that is a stable essence. Instead, it is for the God who is 'beyond the contrast between essence and existence' (1976, 427). Like Berdyaev, Tillich seeks to avoid making God an object. Thus, Tillich will say that God is above being, the ground of being, 'the ontological structure of being', and 'being-it-self' (2012, 210, 265). God should not be thought of as one amongst other beings or a better sort of being, but instead as power, 'the power in everything that has power' (1987, 298). We relate to this power and participate in Being-Itself, and whilst we are not always aware of this, 'we nevertheless accept and participate in it' (2014, 176).

Tillich's comments on the ontological argument help express exactly how. What is important in that argument is not its logical power, but the relationship it expresses between God and the mind. God, as Ultimate Reality, is beyond language and cannot be described in itself, and thus, the ontological argument indicates 'the relation of our mind to Being as such' (1987, 292). It brings out 'an awareness of the infinite is included in man's awareness of finitude. Man knows he is finite, that he is excluded from an infinity which nevertheless belongs to him' (2012, 210). The argument illuminates a lack, a need, and a concern. God, as Being-Itself, is ontologically love, power, and justice and is the 'ultimate reality, the really real, the ground and abyss of everything that is real' (1980, 109). As such, God is 'the subject of all the symbolic statements in which I express my ultimate concern' (1980, 109).

When humanity participates in God, they are able to draw from that power and receive a new kind of being, as the being God itself is engages with and overcomes non-being. God is a dynamic power rather than a static being, this is how 'God is a living God' (2014, 166). The pure power of Being-Itself contains within itself the separation and splits that humanity experiences but without our loss or estrangement. The participation in Being-Itself and its reuniting process is the new paradigm for humanity, rather than conflict and the choice of one's own existence. This power is also love, and the love of God reaches out to estranged and alienated human beings and transforms their existence. It is a dynamic process that 'separates from itself and returns to itself' (1980, 48). This conquers the non-being that pervades human existence, through the process of separation and reunion, through 'Being taking Non-Being into itself' (1980, 49). Whilst we start to participate as individuals in the ground of being, it does not and cannot end there.

Tillich understands his ontology of individualisation in authentic being in God to involve participation in the other. It entails a greater ability to see the other as a person, as able to achieve full personhood. Individuality and relatedness are interdependent for Tillich because of how being is related to the transcendent ground of being, the power that is God. God acts as a guarantee for interpersonal relationships as the unconditioned ground participates in existence and enables one to participate in an other. This interpersonal, interdependent existence, guaranteed through the participation in God, forms the backdrop in which his accounts of love and justice are to be understood. As Tillich writes in *The Courage to Be*, 'perfect self-affirmation is not an isolated act which originates the individual being but is participation in the universal or divine act of self-affirmation, which is the originating power in every individual act' (2014, 23). Through participation in God, we gain, rather than lose, a self, and we encounter the world of others, rather than losing it through isolated self-assertion. This stress on the personal and interpersonal may mitigate somewhat Auden's comment that Tillich presents a God that 'may be the subject of man's concern but can show no concern for men', although it is more debatable whether it meets his point that 'if I try to pray "O Thou Ground, have mercy on me", I start to giggle' (Auden 2015, 230).

Tillich is not keen that we dissolve ourselves either in God or the other, instead stressing the importance of self-affirmation, of healthy self-love and self-centredness that 'is the preservation of this centredness against disruptive tendencies' (1980, 52). Love is not a passive surrender to the power of being, but it is a power that resists and condemns what frustrates the reunion of the separated in divine life (2012, 314, 1980, 114). It is justice in how it 'affirms the independent right of object and subject within the love relation' (2012, 310) ensuring the freedom of the loved one is preserved. Love is absent where there is no individualisation and 'can be fully realised only where there is full individualisation' (2012).

Love then acts as a stabilising influence in our existence and in our being. It is the escape from our ontological estrangement and a move into the true expression of potential being, the New Being. The divine Spirit seeks and strives towards the reunification and consummation of all creatures with the ground of being (1976, 137). The love that is the divine Spirit accepts the existential human and gives the human the knowledge of the transcendent union of essence and existence. This 'spreads healing forces over a personality in all dimensions of his being'; it reunites the ontological elements thus that a 'centred self' emerges (1960). The New Being is thus 're-conciliation, reunion, re-surrection' (1955, 20).

Tillich's thought incorporates the existentialist vision of existence and its ontology but provides an account of the being of God that does not sacrifice freedom nor make being static. Our relation to the being of God is not one of passively accepting an essence or an end, nor is the self dissolved in the expanse of the divine. Instead, the power of God can engage with the impulse we have towards self-creation, with our inability to ground ourselves, and argue that our relationality does not have to be a constant exchange of objectivisation and control. Instead, there exists a ground on which we are able to engage with another.

Although atheistic existentialism accurately articulates the situation of humanity as estranged and anxious, it just leaves us there. Tillich sees that Heidegger diagnoses the problem of existence, but his solution leads to further despair. He carries 'through the Existentialist analysis of the courage to be as oneself more fully than anyone else and, historically speaking, more destructively' (2014, 137). Sartre's statement that 'man is nothing else but what he makes of himself' cuts the self off from others, leading to the loss of the world. Tillich instead proposes a different response to the anxiety and despair that result from the threat of non-being, one that allows for values and ideals other than freedom to ground our ethical and personal relationships with others.

4.4 Conclusion

All three thinkers hold that existence precedes essence, and all see that the being of God coheres with that ontology. Marcel's ontology is fundamentally positive. We start from our existence and are able to go out from there to the positive possibilities that the being of God provides, which do not make us conform to a set essence. Berdyaev's ontology enables there to be a wellspring of positive freedom from which we can source our creativity. We are indeed nothing but what we make of ourselves, and we must make something of ourselves, but doing so is not fulfilling a useless passion but using our creative freedom positively. Tillich's ontology sees that God is not an essence but a constant dynamic movement of separation and reunion. In none of these cases does God restrict human existence. Instead, God provides the means by which human existence can transcend and transcend positively rather than futilely. Having argued that these thinkers, who all espouse monotheism, can be classed as existentialists proper, I turn to a more direct comparison of the atheistic existentialists with these Christian existentialists. Through this comparison, I will come to several conclusions about the relationship between existentialism and monotheism.

5 Monotheism and Existentialism, Evaluated

Whilst the existentialist slogan that existence precedes essence has often been taken to exclude monotheism, I have argued that it need not. Seeing this statement as an ontological claim has opened up the possibility of a new account of the relation between humanity and God. It allows for new perspectives on how to define existentialism and shows the theistic potentiality of a claim that, at first blush, appears implicitly atheistic. This opens up ways of understanding existentialism that are not as dependent on the genealogy of existentialism, or the outworkings of authenticity. It has shown that this central slogan of existentialism is not *de facto* atheistic but can be used theistically. In doing so, it expands how we can conceive of existentialist relationality, ethics, and ontology.

This approach enables a fuller consideration of monotheistic existentialists as existentialists proper. They, as much as the atheistic existentialists, grapple with the ontological, metaphysical, relational, and ethical implications of having existence precede essence. The claim that existence precedes essence entails reflection on that for the being of God as well as for humanity. Thus, there can be fruitful grounds on which to discuss existentialist themes in relation to monotheism. To do is not an imposition of a foreign ontology, neither is it altering the character of existentialism such that it ceases to be existentialism. The monotheistic thinkers, in grappling with the statement that existence precedes essence, are able to talk of non-being and being in God, and none hold to the static ideal of the in-itself-for-itself that Sartre finds impossible. I turn now to explore three connected themes that are affected by the statement that existence precedes essence. In doing so, I will relate the later ethics of Sartre and Beauvoir to monotheism, critically and constructively. Through this comparison, I will argue that theistic existentialists can provide ontological frameworks and ethical options that Sartre and Beauvoir may profess but cannot justify.

5.1 Ontology and Relationality

In *Being and Nothingness*, part of Sartre's broadside against the existence of God concerns how God could be used to support our relationships with other people. Perhaps we could have God as the mediator between the self and other and have God ground that relationship. Sartre's criticism of this point is that rooting ourselves and the other in the being of God only means that other people underscore the impossibility of the idea of God. He writes that 'if God is I and if he is the Other, then what guarantees my own existence?' If God were to exist as the intermediary between me and another, that already presupposes 'the presence of the Other to me in an internal connection'. Either God is superfluous, as I already have the connection to the other, or impossible, God 'must be able to maintain an internal connection with myself in order for a real foundation of the Other's existence to be valid for me' (Sartre 1992, 232).

However, this is a vision of God and God's grounding of relationality that does not necessarily engage with the way in which monotheistic existentialists see God as grounding and enabling interpersonal relationships. And this does revolve around the limits that Sartre sets himself in having existence precede essence. As Marcel, Berdyaev, and Tillich show, there are ways of construing existence and essence and their order such that God can ground but not overdetermine, overbear, or make superfluous, our relationships with others.

As noted earlier, Sartre's own view of freedom and thus relationality changes throughout his work. In 'Existentialism is a Humanism', the existentialist mandate and vision go beyond the self and its objectifying relationships. When the individual chooses 'for himself he chooses for all men' (1948, 29). Our choices are individual, but they are not necessarily objectifying, instead they affirm our relationality. Here, we bear the responsibility for what humanity is and should be: it is a statement on the existence of others. This melds with Beauvoir's sedimented freedom such that we are projects that become built up. Through this, we are able to relate more positively towards the other, to have a shape for their lives, and to act towards them in such a way as to increase their freedom.

This is underscored by the ontology of existence preceding essence: only through this can our choices make humanity this kind of project. This further underscores how Camus's philosophy should not be considered existentialist, as in his vision of human nature and duty, he does not envision it through these lenses. Instead, he affirms humanity, despite his many doubts, and proposes a more set humanism, albeit one that looks back nervously over its shoulder.

Yet their more positive, responsible view of freedom occurs in an ontological vacuum, as Berdyaev and Tillich note. Tillich and Marcel in particular understand the human being as related to God in such a way that our sedimentation and project takes from God and is grounded in God, rather than in our own self-supported projects, acts, and failures. Berdyaev's meontic freedom relies on a particular ontology such that freedom can remain nothingness but be a kind of nothingness that has positive potentiality rather than being parasitic. They can therefore formulate an account of human being where existence precedes essence, and this existence is aided, rather than limited, by God. They allow for an ontological account of the self and the other where authenticity and relationality are consistent, not contradictory.

The ontological lack in Sartre and ontological possibilities in monotheistic existentialism can also open up existentialism proper to contemporary explorations of postmodern metaphysics. Whilst not all of these thinkers specifically take up the question of God and metaphysics as articulated by Heidegger's critique of onto-theology, they can provide accounts of both God and humanity that continue to be relevant to these contemporary discussions.

5.2 Activity and Passivity

As regards the ontological claims of existence and essence, the rejection of monotheism in claiming that existence precedes essence is a rejection of passivity in human nature. This then makes freedom dependent on that exercise of authenticity. As we have seen, existentialism has been classified as a practical tradition of personal authenticity. Of the theistic existentialists, Berdyaev comes closest to also being able to endorse this: the meontic freedom that is part of our being must be exercised, we have this drive to create. Yet there is not the same sense in Berdyaev as there is in Sartre that freedom is the rejection of grace or passivity. Berdyaev's thought, whilst embracing and almost mandating this activity, is not alien or opposed to grace. Whilst, as Tillich remarks, we cannot regain the ontological stability of Augustine, the ontologies of God and the human can be reconfigured in such a way that our being can be built up, and a different kind of ontological stability can be achieved. Marcel, especially, and Tillich, to an extent, also have a dialectic of passivity and activity, rather than seeing passivity in relation to God always as a particularly pronounced form of bad faith.

How the being of God is brought into the conversation around existence preceding essence makes this possible. As detailed by the aforementioned theistic existentialists, the being of God can ground and reinvigorate being without limiting and determining it any more than Sartre and Beauvoir do. There can also be positive relationships with the world and with others in the world by drawing on that being of God. This movement is found in all three monotheistic existentialists and explored in different ways. But Beauvoir and Sartre's ontology, in rejecting the idea of God and having the wellspring of freedom be a lack, has to constantly resist anything from outside the self that could benefit the self. They have to resist passivity in favour of this active engagement and relationship to the world. This is despite their later alignments with particular political ideals and ends, as well as the way in which freedom is then used to be a guiding ideal in their thought, something that we seek to arrange for others. This focus on activity is based around the ontological impossibility of passivity in their thought. Here, the tenet that existence precedes essence hinders their thought, rather than opening up the glorious but dreadful freedom that Sartre promises in 'Existentialism is a Humanism'.

5.3 Freedom and Responsibility

Although Sartre's views on freedom and interpersonal relationships shift from *Being and Nothingness* through 'Existentialism is a Humanism' and his later works, *Saint Genet* and *The Anti-Semite and the Jew*, he always hedges an ethics, never setting out the system that could correspond to his ontology. Webber sees that the radical freedom of a God is abandoned when Sartre comes to write *Saint Genet*. There it is more in line with Beauvoir's conception of it, where 'freedom consists in the ability to commit to projects that shape one's outlook and that sedimentation is essential to such commitment' (Webber 2018, 5). Whilst in *Saint Genet* there is still the lovelessness that is 'the direct result of personhood in freedom' (Kirkpatrick 2019, 23), there is, from Beauvoir, the possibility of reciprocity. In her work on freedom and responsibility, Beauvoir rejects an absolute form of ethics in favour of Montaigne's epitaph that 'life in itself is neither good nor evil. It is the place of good and evil, according to what you make it'. Yet there is still a constant mandate and drive here that we should always seek the liberation of ourselves and others, caught as we are in our ambiguity and its tension, with morality 'residing in the painfulness of an indefinite questioning' (Beauvoir 2018, 133).

Even with the more sedimented freedom, the existentialist stress on the individual raises questions of how to move from the individual and their subjective authenticity to others and their authenticity. This then further raises questions of how to ethically engage with the other such that their authenticity can be preserved. In Beauvoir, it has to remain unsolvable; our ethics remain ambiguous for there can be no set content to them. However, there is still the goal of freedom and our ethical mandate to increase its boundaries and presence.

Yet it does seem that freedom is swapped in for God. In doing so, the problems raised by having such a goal and end as discussed in Sartre's *Being and Nothingness* are elided. Why should freedom become the kind of existence that we wish for others? What is the content of freedom that means it is different from the desire to be God? Perhaps, as freedom is our nothingness, it is not limiting in the way that love, being, and the in-itself-for-itself would be. Yet, by this stage, freedom itself is not the freedom of a God but something more limited, sedimented, and situated. How exactly is this freedom, both for ourselves and for others, not itself an impossibility, and our drive towards it not another useless passion? The focus, drive, and mandate towards freedom may be just as much bad faith as anything else.

I believe there are two concerns here. First, if we follow existence preceding essence as understood by the atheistic existentialists, it is not a robust enough ontological framework to support what they want freedom to do. They must either remain in an ontological impossibility concerning freedom and relationality or write cheques that their ontology cannot cash. The second is that freedom takes on the role God had in previous thought, and potential problems are elided in the process. I hesitate to say that Sartre and Beauvoir's problems are resolved by monotheism: for them, that would involve several kinds of bad faith, but the ethical and communal visions of the monotheistic existentialists allow for more content than can be found otherwise. However, as we have explored, that requires a different ontological framework.

5.4 A Final Reflection

This Element has advanced several arguments. The first is that one of the key ways in which to define existentialism, as dependent on the ontological claim that existence precedes essence, does not mean that existentialism is *de jure* atheistic, or that God is necessarily *de trop* – or at least not any more than existence itself is. Instead, existentialism and monotheism are not only not exclusionary concepts but are also in fact compatible. The second is that the tenet that existence precedes essence is productive for new understandings of monotheism and humanity. There are new options for human relationality and new possibilities for ethical relationships to be formulated. The formula that existence precedes essence supports, rather than undermines these, and it opens up ways in which to relate monotheism to contemporary concerns.

Another is that this view contests the judgement that human freedom and authentic existence are impossible in relation to God. This text has shown that existentialism's understanding of freedom and authenticity is linked to and formed in relation to monotheism. Whilst it initially appears that existentialism proper reacts against monotheism, it in fact draws on monotheism in order to provide content to its account of freedom. Indeed, freedom, authenticity, and the individual are just as important to monotheistic as to atheistic existentialism. Monotheistic accounts of existentialism are able, even with existence preceding essence, to promote a more relational ontology that does not sacrifice freedom, authenticity, and the individual, but can frame and structure them more cohesively.

This study has focused in detail on six thinkers associated with atheistic and monotheistic existentialism. Due to the breadth of the existentialist umbrella, the height and span of the existentialist tree, and the applicability of the paradigm that existence precedes essence, many more thinkers, atheistic and monotheistic, are ripe for inclusion and discussion. The existence of God does indeed make a difference for the existentialist, who can be even more optimistic: with more grounds for action and further ways to hope.

References

Archambault, Paul. (1972) *Camus' Hellenic Sources*. Chapel Hill: University of North Carolina Press.

Aronson, Raymond (2012) 'Camus the Unbeliever: Living without God', in *Situating Existentialism: Key Texts in Context*, ed. Jonathan Judaken and Robert Bernasconi. New York: Columbia University Press, 256–276.

Auden, W. H. (2015) *The Complete Works of W. H. Auden: Prose*, vol. 5, 1963–1968. Princeton: Princeton University Press.

Augustine (2003) *City of God*, trans. Henry Bettenson. London: Penguin. (1961) *Confessions*, trans. R. S. Pine-Coffin. London: Penguin.

Baring, Edward (2015) 'Anxiety in Translation: Naming Existentialism before Sartre'. *History of European Ideas* 41, no. 4: 470–488.

Barrett, William (1958) *Irrational Man: A Study in Existentialist Philosophy*. New York: Doubleday.

Beauvoir, Simone de (2006) *Diary of a Philosophy Student*, vol. 1, 1926–27, ed. Barbara Klaw et al. Chicago: University of Illinois Press.

(2018) *The Ethics of Ambiguity*. New York: Open Road.

(2004[1945]) 'Existentialism and Popular Wisdom', in *Simone de Beauvoir: Philosophical Writings*, ed. Margaret Simons with Mary Beth Timmerman and Mary Beth Mader. Chicago: University of Illinois Press., 195-220

(1962) *The Prime of Life*, trans. Peter Green. London: Penguin.

(2004[1944]) 'Pyrrhus and Cineas', in *Simone de Beauvoir: Philosophical Writings*, ed. Margaret Simons with Mary Beth Timmerman and Mary Beth Mader. Chicago: University of Illinois Press., 77-150

(2004[1947]) 'What is Existentialism?', in *Simone de Beauvoir: Philosophical Writings*, ed. Margaret Simons with Mary Beth Timmerman and Mary Beth Mader. Chicago: University of Illinois Press., 317-326

Berdyaev, Nicholas (1960) *The Destiny of Man*, trans. Natalie Duddington. New York: Harper and Brothers.

(1949) *The Divine and the Human*, trans. R. M. French. London: Geoffrey Bles.

(1950) *Dream and Reality: An Essay in Autobiography*, trans. K. Lampert. London: Geoffrey Bles.

(1962) *The Meaning of the Creative Act*, trans. Donald M. Lowrie. New York: Collier Books.

(1947) *Solitude and Society*, trans. George Reavey. London: Geoffrey Bles.

(1939) *Spirit and Reality*, trans. George Reavey. London: Geoffrey Bles.

(1949) *Towards a New Epoch*, trans. Oliver Fielding Clarke. London: Geoffrey Bles.

(1953) *Truth and Revelation*, trans. R. M. French. London: Geoffrey Bles.

Camus, Albert (2007) *Christian Metaphysics and Neoplatonism*, trans. Intro. Ronald D. Srigley. Columbia: University of Missouri Press.

(1956) *La Chute*. Paris: Gallimard.

(1951) *L'Homme Revolté*. Paris: Gallimard.

(1970) *Lyrical and Critical Essays*, ed. Philip Thody. New York: Vintage.

(1964) *The Myth of Sisyphus and Other Essays*. New York: Knopf.

(1963) *Notebooks 1935–42*, trans. Philip Thody. New York: Knopf.

(1966) *Notebooks 1942–1951*, trans. Justin O'Brien. New York: Knopf.

(2008) *Notebooks 1951–1959*, trans. Ryan Bloom. Chicago: Ivan Dee.

Cavell, Stanley (1979) *The Claim of Reason*. Oxford: Oxford University Press.

Cochrane, Arthur (1956) *The Existentialists and God*. Philadelphia: The Westminster Press.

Contat, Michel and Michel Rybalka (1974) *The Writings of Jean-Paul Sartre*. Evanston: Northwestern University Press.

Cooper, David E. (1990) *Existentialism: A Reconstruction*. Oxford: Blackwell.

(2012) 'Existentialism as a Philosophical Movement', in *The Cambridge Companion to Existentialism*, ed. Steven Crowell. Cambridge: Cambridge University Press, 27–49.

Crowell, Steven (2012) 'Existentialism and Its Legacy'. *The Cambridge Companion to Existentialism*. Cambridge: Cambridge University Press.

(2020) 'Existentialism', in *The Stanford Encyclopedia of Philosophy*, ed. Edward N. Zalta. https://plato.stanford.edu/archives/sum2020/entries/existentialism/.

Cruickshank, John (1967) 'Albert Camus: Sainthood without God', in *Mansions of the Spirit: Essays in Literature and Religion*, ed. George A. Panichas. New York: Hawthorn, 313–324.

(1957) 'Existentialism after Twelve Years: An Evaluation'. *Dublin Review* 231: 52–65.

Desan, Wilfrid (1954) *The Tragic Finale: An Essay on the Philosophy of Jean-Paul Sartre*. New York: Harper and Row.

Descombes, Vincent (1991) 'Le Moment français de Nietzsche', in *Pourquoi nous ne sommes pas nietzschéens*, ed. Alain Boyer et al. Paris: Grasset.

Dreyfus, Hubert L. (2006) 'The Roots of Existentialism', in *A Companion to Phenomenology and Existentialism*, ed. Hubert L. Dreyfus and Mark A. Wrathall. Oxford: Blackwell, 136–161.

Dreyfus, Hubert L. and Mark A. Wrathall, eds. (2006) *A Companion to Phenomenology and Existentialism*. Oxford: Blackwell.

Earnshaw, Steven (2006) *Existentialism: A Guide for the Perplexed*. London: Continuum.

Flynn, Thomas (2006) *Existentialism: A Very Short Introduction*. Oxford: Oxford University Press.

Grene, Marjorie (1948) *Dreadful Freedom: A Critique of Existentialism*. Chicago: University of Chicago Press.

Grimsley, Ronald (1960) *Existentialist Thought*, 2nd ed. Cardiff: University of Wales Press.

Hadot, Pierre (1995) *Philosophy as a Way of Life*. Oxford: Blackwell.

Heidegger, Martin (2008) *Basic Writings*, trans. David Farell Krell and Taylor Carman. Abingdon: Routledge.

(1962) *Being and Time*, trans. John Macquarrie and Edward Robinson. New York: Harper.

(1969) *Identity and Difference*, trans. Joan Staumburgh. New York: Harper and Row.

(2006) *Mindfulness*, trans. Parvis Emad and Thomas Kalary. London: Athlone.

(2004) *The Phenomenology of Religious Life*, trans. Matthias Fritsch and Jennifer Anna Gosetti-Ferencei. Bloomington: Indiana University Press.

(1977) *The Question Concerning Technology and Other Essays*, trans. William Lovitt. New York: Garland.

Jaspers, Karl (1969) *Philosophy*, vol. 1, trans. E. B. Ashton. Chicago: University of Chicago Press.

(1970) *Philosophy*, vol. 2, trans. E. B. Ashton. Chicago: University of Chicago Press.

(1971a) *Philosophy*, vol. 3, trans. E. B. Ashton. Chicago: University of Chicago Press.

(1971b) *Philosophy of Existence*, trans. R. F. Grabau. Philadelphia: University of Pennsylvania Press.

(1955) *Reason and Existenz*, trans. William Earle. New York: Noonday Press.

Joseph, Felicity, Jack Reynolds, and Ashley Woodward, eds. (2011) 'Introduction', in *The Continuum Companion to Existentialism*. London: Continuum, 1–14.

Judaken, Jonathan (2012) 'Introduction', in *Situating Existentialism: Key Texts in Context*, ed. Jonathan Judaken and Robert Bernasconi. New York: Columbia University Press, 1–34.

Judaken, Jonathan and Robert Bernasconi, eds. (2012) *Situating Existentialism: Key Texts in Context*. New York: Columbia University Press.

Kaufmann, Walter (1995) *Existentialism: From Dostoevsky to Sartre*. New York: Meridian Books.

Khawaja, Noreen (2016) *The Religion of Existence: Asceticism in Philosophy from Kierkegaard to Sartre*. Chicago: University of Chicago Press.

Kierkegaard, Søren (1980) *The Concept of Anxiety*, trans. Reidar Thomte. Princeton: Princeton University Press.

   (1982) *Concluding Unscientific Postscript*, vol. 1, trans. Howard V. Hong and Edna H. Hong. Princeton: Princeton University Press.

   (1983) *The Sickness unto Death*, trans. Howard V. Hong and Edna H. Hong. Princeton: Princeton University Press.

   (1967–1978) *Søren Kierkegaard's Journals and Papers*, trans. Howard V. Hong and Edna H. Hong. Bloomington: Indiana University Press.

Kirkpatrick, Kate (2019) 'Master, Slave and Merciless Struggle'. *Sartre Studies International* 25, no. 1: 22–34.

   (2017) *Sartre on Sin: Between Being and Nothingness*. Oxford: Oxford University Press.

Kirkpatrick, Kate and George Pattison (2018) *The Mystical Sources of Existentialist Thought: Being, Nothingness, Love*. London: Routledge.

Macquarrie, John (1955) *An Existential Theology*. London: SCM Press.

   (1972) *Existentialism: An Introduction, Guide, and Assessment*. Harmondsworth: Penguin. 1

Mahon, Joseph (2002) *Simone de Beauvoir and Her Catholicism: An Essay on Her Ethical and Religious Meditations*. Arlen House.

Malpas, Jeff (2012) 'Existentialism as Literature', in *The Cambridge Companion to Existentialism*, ed. Steven Crowell. Cambridge: Cambridge University Press, 291–321.

Marcel, Gabriel (1984) 'An Autobiographical Essay', in *The Philosophy of Gabriel Marcel*, ed. Paul Arthur Schilpp and Lewis Edwin Hahn. Carbondale: Open Court, 3–68.

   (1949) *Being and Having*, trans. Katharine Farrer. Westminster: Dacre Press.

   (1964) *Creative Fidelity*, trans. Robert Rosthal. New York: Farrar, Strauss.

   (1962) *Homo Viator: Introduction to a Metaphysic of Hope*, trans. Emma Crawford. New York: Harper Torchbooks.

   (1951) *The Mystery of Being, vol. 1, Reflection and Mystery*, trans. G. S. Fraser. London: The Harvill Press.

Martin, Clancy (2006) 'Religious Existentialism', in *A Companion to Phenomenology and Existentialism*, ed. Hubert L. Dreyfus and Mark A. Wrathall. Oxford: Blackwell, 188–205.

McBride, Joseph (1992) *Albert Camus: Philosopher and Littérateur.* New York: St. Martin's Press.

McBride, William (2012) 'Existentialism as a Cultural Movement', in *The Cambridge Companion to Existentialism*, ed. Steven Crowell. Cambridge: Cambridge University Press, 50–72.

Merleau-Ponty, Maurice (1945) *Phénoménologie de la perception.* Paris: Gallimard.

Michalski, Krzysztof (2013) *The Flame of Eternity: An Interpretation of Nietzsche's Thought.* Princeton: Princeton University Press.

Mounier, Emanuel (1946) *Introduction aux existentialismes.* Paris: Gallimard.

Mulhall, Stephen (2005) *Philosophical Myths of the Fall.* Princeton: Princeton University Press.

Murdoch, Iris (1999) *Existentialists and Mystics.* London: Penguin.

Nietzsche, Friedrich (1993) *The Birth of Tragedy,* trans. Shaun Whiteside. London: Penguin.

(2006) *The Genealogy of Morals and Other Writings*, ed. Keith Ansell-Pearson, trans. Carol Diethe. Cambridge: Cambridge University Press.

(1996) *Human, All too Human: A Book for Free Spirits*, ed. R. J. Hollingdale. Cambridge: Cambridge University Press.

(2001a) *Nietzsche: Beyond Good and Evil: Prelude to a Philosophy of the Future*, ed. Rolf-Peter Horstmann and Judith Norman. Cambridge: Cambridge University Press.

(2001b) *Nietzsche: The Gay Science: With a Prelude in German Rhymes and an Appendix of Songs*, ed. Bernard Williams, trans. Josefine Nauckhoff and Adrian Del Caro. Cambridge: Cambridge University Press.

(1969) *Thus Spake Zarathustra.* New York: Random House.

(1990) *Twilight of the Idols and the Anti-Christ: Or How to Philosophize with a Hammer*, ed. Michael Tanner, trans. R. J. Hollingdale. London: Penguin.

(1968) *The Will to Power*, trans. Walter Kaufmann. New York: Vintage Books.

Paffenroth, Kim, John Doody, and Helene Tallon Russell, eds. (2017) *Augustine and Kierkegaard.* Lanham: Rowman and Littlefield.

Pascal, Blaise (1995) *Pensées and Other Writings*, trans. Honor Levi. Oxford: Oxford University Press.

Pattison, George (1999) *Anxious Angels: A Retrospective View of Religious Existentialism.* Hampshire: Macmillan.

(2020) 'Berdyaev and Christian Existentialism', in *Oxford Handbook to Russian Religious Thought*, ed. George Pattison, Caryl Emerson, and Randall A. Poole . Oxford: Oxford University Press. 450–463.

(2015) *Paul Tillich's Philosophical Theology: A Fifty Year Reappraisal.* London: Palgrave Macmillan.

Pax, Clyde (1972) *An Existential Approach to God: A Study of Gabriel Marcel.* The Hague: Martinus Nijhoff.

Reynolds, Jack (2006) *Understanding Existentialism.* Durham: Acumen.

Sartre, Jean-Paul (1992) *Being and Nothingness*, trans. Hazel Barnes. New York: Washington Square Press.

(1948) *Existentialism and Humanism*, trans. Philip Mairet. London: Butler and Tanner.

(1938) *La Nausée.* Paris: Gallimard.

(2010) 'A New Mystic', in *Critical Essays*, trans. Chris Turner. London: Seagull Books.

(1976) *No Exit and Three Other Plays.* New York: Vintage International.

(1952) 'Réponse à Albert Camus'. *Les Temps Modernes* 82: 334–353.

(1960) *The Transcendence of the Ego: An Existentialist Theory of Consciousness*, ed. and trans. Forrest Williams and Robert Kirkpatrick. New York: Hill and Wang.

Schacht, Richard (2012) 'Nietzsche: After the Death of God' in *The Cambridge Companion to Existentialism*, ed. Steven Crowell. Cambridge University Press, 111–136.

Schelling, Friedrich (1989) *Historical-Critical Introduction to the Philosophy of Mythology*, trans. Mason Richey and Marcus Zisselsberger. Albany: State University of New York Press.

Sharpe, Matthew, Maciej Kałuża, and Peter Francev, eds. (2020) *Brill's Companion to Camus: Camus among the Philosophers.* Leiden: Brill.

Solomon, Robert C., ed. (1974) *Existentialism.* New York: Modern Library.

Sprintzen, David (2020) 'Sartre and Camus: A Much-Misunderstood Relationship', in *Brill's Companion to Camus: Camus among the Philosophers*, ed. Matthew Sharpe, Maciej Kałuża, and Peter Francev. Leiden: Brill, 248–268.

Ronald D. Srigley (2007). 'Intro' in *Christian Metaphysics and Neoplatonism*, ed. Albert Camus. Columbia: University of Missouri Press.

Stewart, Jon (2010) *Idealism and Existentialism.* London: Continuum.

Teboul, Margaret (2005) 'La réception de Kierkegaard en France 1930–1960'. *Revue des sciences philosophiques et théologiques* 89, no. 2: 315–336.

Tillich, Paul (2014) *The Courage to Be.* New Haven: Yale University Press.

(1960) 'The Impact of Psychotherapy on Theological Thought'. *Pastoral Psychology* 11: 17–23.

(1980) *Love, Power, and Justice.* New York: Oxford University Press.

(1955) *The New Being.* New York: Scribner.

(2012) *Systematic Theology*, vol. 1. Chicago: University of Chicago Press.

(2013) *Systematic Theology*, vol. 2. Chicago: University of Chicago Press.

(1976) *Systematic Theology*, vol. 3. Chicago: University of Chicago Press.

(1987) 'The Two Types of Philosophy of Religion', in *Writings in the Philosophy of Religion: Main Works*, vol. 4, ed. John Clayton. Berlin: De Gruyter, 289–300.

Wahl, Jean (1969) *Philosophies of Existence: An Introduction to the Basic Thought of Kierkegaard, Heidegger, Jaspers, Marcel, Sartre*. London: Routledge.

(1949) *A Short History of Existentialism*. New York: Philosophical Library.

Warnock, Mary (1970) *Existentialism*. Oxford: Oxford University Press.

(1967) *Existentialist Ethics*. London: Macmillan.

Webber, Jonathan (2009) *The Existentialism of Jean-Paul Sartre*. London: Routledge.

(2018) *Rethinking Existentialism*. Oxford: Oxford University Press.

Westphal, Merold (2012) 'Existentialism and Religion', in *The Cambridge Companion to Existentialism*, ed. Steven Crowell. Cambridge: Cambridge University Press, 322–341.

Whistler, Grace (2018) '"Saints without God": Camus's Poetics of Secular Faith'. *Nordisk Judaistik Scandinavian Jewish Studies* 29, no. 1: 49–61.

Acknowledgements

It seemed a good idea at the time, that time being January 2021, to start intensively working on existentialism. For the opportunity to have done so and for their support, correction, and comments, I am deeply grateful to the editors of this series, Paul Moser and Chad Meister. I am thankful also for the helpful comments of the two external reviewers, and for their time and attention to the text. I am further immensely grateful to Kate Kirkpatrick and King-Ho Leung for their comments on the manuscript.

As the various lockdowns in Germany continued under their various names and in their varying intensities, I find myself utterly grateful and deeply indebted in particular to Alex Englander, Franca Hoffmann, and Niels Martens for their friendship, support, and distraction. Michael Schulz, Jakob Höfting, and David Engelbarth at the Arbeitsbereich für Philosophie und Theorie der Religionen at the University of Bonn further made this project, and my own, more enjoyable than appearances suggest. If it is the case that we are thrown into existence and forced to make a project of ourselves, then I am fortunate indeed not only in my freedom but also in my facticity. So, as a certain writer on nausea once said: let's get on with it.

Cambridge Elements $\overline{\overline{=}}$

Religion and Monotheism

Paul K. Moser
Loyola University Chicago

Paul K. Moser is Professor of Philosophy at Loyola University Chicago. He is the author of *Understanding Religious Experience; The God Relationship; The Elusive God* (winner of national book award from the Jesuit Honor Society); *The Evidence for God; The Severity of God; Knowledge and Evidence (*all Cambridge University Press); and *Philosophy after Objectivity* (Oxford University Press); co-author of *Theory of Knowledge* (Oxford University Press); editor of *Jesus and Philosophy* (Cambridge University Press) and *The Oxford Handbook of Epistemology* (Oxford University Press); co-editor of *The Wisdom of the Christian Faith (*Cambridge University Press). He is the co-editor with Chad Meister of the book series *Cambridge Studies in Religion, Philosophy, and Society.*

Chad Meister
Bethel University

Chad Meister is Professor of Philosophy and Theology and Department Chair at Bethel College. He is the author of *Introducing Philosophy of Religion* (Routledge, 2009), *Christian Thought: A Historical Introduction*, 2nd edition (Routledge, 2017), and *Evil: A Guide for the Perplexed*, 2nd edition (Bloomsbury, 2018). He has edited or co-edited the following: *The Oxford Handbook of Religious Diversity* (Oxford University Press, 2010), *Debating Christian Theism* (Oxford University Press, 2011), with Paul Moser, *The Cambridge Companion to the Problem of Evil* (Cambridge University Press, 2017), and with Charles Taliaferro, *The History of Evil* (Routledge 2018, in six volumes).

About the Series

This Cambridge Element series publishes original concise volumes on monotheism and its significance. Monotheism has occupied inquirers since the time of the Biblical patriarch, and it continues to attract interdisciplinary academic work today. Engaging, current, and concise, the Elements benefit teachers, researched, and advanced students in religious studies, Biblical studies, theology, philosophy of religion, and related fields.

Cambridge Elements ⁼

Religion and Monotheism

Elements in the Series

Monotheism and the Meaning of Life
T. J. Mawson

Monotheism and Contemporary Atheism
Michael Ruse

Monotheism and Hope in God
William J. Wainwright

Monotheism and Religious Diversity
Roger Trigg

Divine Ideas
Thomas M. Ward

Hindu Monotheism
Gavin Dennis Flood

Monotheism and the Rise of Science
J. L. Schellenberg

Monotheism and Faith in God
Ian G. Wallis

Monotheism and Human Nature
Andrew M. Bailey

Monotheism and Forgiveness
S. Mark Heim

Monotheism, Biblical Traditions, and Race Relations
Yung Suk Kim

Monotheism and Existentialism
Deborah Casewell

A full series listing is available at: www.cambridge.org/er&m

Printed in the United States
by Baker & Taylor Publisher Services